Happy holidays Nadine!

You are an amazing Teammate and the team is a better place with you on it. Thank you ♡

Stay safe,
Love Gabriella Griffin/Griff

Boathouse Row
COOKBOOK

Izzie Brown, MS, RD

Copyright © 2011 by Izzie Brown
All rights reserved.
ISBN-13: 978-1468055993
ISBN-10: 1468055992

Dedication

To Fred, whose love of rowing is outpaced
only by his fortitude and good humor.

Expressions of Appreciation

To Clete Graham for his unwavering optimism and willingness to say "yes".

To Ozan Berke for his design, layout and typesetting skills.

To Barry Lewis for his keen photographic eye.

To Charles, Gabby and Juliana for their endless love and support.

Special Thanks

To Edith Duling, Margaret Tobin and Corbin Brown, this book would not have happened without them.

To all of you who participated in the recipe donation drive. Your generosity and caring is deeply appreciated.

To all of you who purchased the book in support of Fred Duling, Sr.

I hope that you will use the recipes often and treasure the cookbook as a keepsake representing both the society and culture of rowing.

Recipe of a Rower

1 heaping cup of tenacity
Equal parts dedication and commitment
¾ cup laughter and smiles
½ cup patience
¼ cup grit
Pinch of hedonism
Twist of narcissism
Mix ingredients well
Toss over peaceful dawns and sun-streaked dusks
Serve with enthusiasm. Bon Appétit.

Editor's Notes

In a few instances I altered recipes with the intent to include more healthful ingredients.

I substituted butter for margarine, as many brands of margarine are made with "partially hydrogenated" oil. A "fully hydrogenated" or simply "hydrogenated" margarine, however, would be acceptable.

When cooking with oil, choose canola oil over all other vegetable oils including olive. If using oils in uncooked recipes, canola or olive oil is best, letting taste guide your decision.

I tried to use all the recipes received and regret if there are any errors or omissions.

About The History

My intent with the subsequent history was to compile, in one location, a brief history of each club comprising Boathouse Row. While I tried to be thorough and document my sources, many elements of the evolution of Boathouse Row are missing. Using personal communications, historic publications (both online and printed), individual boathouse websites and Wikipedia, the following descriptions were created.

As I uncovered information about the clubs and boathouses, answers to some questions were revealed but other questions arose. For example, you may find that there is great detail about some clubs or buildings and little detail about others. This is not an intentional omission but purely a representation of what I could find. I hope that a more ambitious historian will incorporate what I found into a more complete documentation of the clubs of Boathouse Row.

May your boat move quietly and swiftly,

Izzie

Observations and Interpretations

Based solely on the numbers and varieties of recipes submitted, interpretations about the way rowers eat could be made.

1. Rowers eat breakfast! ☺
2. Rowers like fish and poultry! ☺
3. Rowers like pasta in all shapes! ☺
4. Rowers spend little time preparing and eating vegetables! ☹
5. While rowers eat bread and rolls, they don't generally bake them
6. While rowers eat appetizers, side dishes and soups, they do so less often than main dishes and desserts
7. Rowers like dessert! And chocolate is hands-down, the ingredient of choice

Happy cooking and happier eating!

Recipe Icons

Kid-Friendly   *Quick & Easy*   *Heart-Healthy*   *Freezes Well*   *Spicy*   *Vegetarian*

Contents

Runner's World Article by Amby Burfoot 10

The History of Boathouse Row 16

The Boathouses 20

Hearty Breakfasts 34

On-The-Go 41

Appetizers 46

Breads and Rolls 53

Salads 56

Vegetables and Side Dishes 64

Soups & Stews 76

Main Dishes 89

Desserts 125

Stocks, Sauces and Dressings 162

Kitchen Helper 171

Fred Duling Aims For His 52nd Straight Thanksgiving-Day Race Finish. Only This One Is Different.

November 20, 2011
By Amby Burfoot

This article originally appeared on www.runnersworld.com. Republished with the permission of Rodale Inc.

I've heard a lot of amazing stories in my 50 years of running, and 33 years of running journalism. This one takes the cake.

There are a number of things you should understand about Fred Duling, more than I can possibly recount here, but let's give it a try. First and foremost, he's a rower–a Schuylkill River rower to be precise. That's a special family–hardy, tradition-draped, and renowned across the globe. Duling has rowed on three U.S. national teams and won enough age-group competitions to put him in Ed Whitlock territory.

Many rowers like to do a little running to stay in shape after the season, and Duling has been down that road. He's never been the fastest kid on the block–he's a rower, remember–but you'd have to say he's got pretty good endurance and consistency. Last Thanksgiving he finished the 107th Schuylkill Navy Run (about 5.6 miles) in 47:46. It was his 51st consecutive finish in the race, mostly a competition among local rowers.

That gives Duling the oldest active race streak in the country. Phil Smith hit 50 straight at Dipsea in 2010, but chose to sit out the 2011 Dipsea. I'll be aiming for my 49th straight at Manchester CT on Thanksgiving Day. That gives Duling a whopping three-year edge on me.

How does a guy piece together 51-going-on-52 straight years in the same race?

"Fred's a bad ass," says one of his many admirers along Philadelphia's boathouse row. "He's one tough old son-of-a-_____," says his best friend Clete Graham, rower and organizer of the Schuykill Navy Run. These are gross understatements, as you'll soon understand.

Less than two weeks after last Thanksgiving, Fred was alone in his beloved Malta

Boat Club, decorating the club's Christmas tree. It was a tall tree; Fred was up on a ladder. To this date, no one knows what happened. When found, Fred was crumpled immobile on the floor, his body temperature 86, and his spine fractured in multiple places. (You can get more than enough medical details at PullForFred.com). Only one part of his body was left unscathed: his fighting spirit.

Fred has been in intensive care units, rehab hospitals, and wheelchairs ever since. He's paralyzed from the abdomen down. Accidents this severe don't lend themselves to smooth recoveries, and Fred has had his share of ups and downs in the last 12 months.

But Thursday morning, Fred will be on the Navy Run start line again, same as the last 51 years. Only this time, Clete Graham will give Fred a quarter-mile head start to make sure he gets a clean glide off the line. And Fred's daughter Sara will be adding a little push on the steepest, grassiest parts of the course, which includes a couple of miles of cross-country terrain. "He'll make it, the same as always," says Graham. "He's just so competitive, and he's got such an attitude of going-for it."

Afterwards, Fred, the unofficial assistant race director to Graham's number-one position, will help with the awards ceremony. He will have picked up the awards the day before; now he'll hand them out to the various category winners. The same as always.

Except, perhaps for this: At the 108th Schuylkill Navy Run, it won't mean much to be a category winner. Because no matter how fast you are, or what your age group, you don't begin to compare to the most-amazing athlete in the race.

That, of course, would be the winner of the Bad Ass prize. That would be Fred Duling.

Below, Fred Duling's 28-year old daughter Sara answers a few questions about her Dad.

How did your Dad get so tough?
I know some people can point to one moment or person in their life as their source of inspiration, what keeps them driving along. I don't think that is true for my Dad, I think that it is the sum of his experiences. At the end of the day he has a "just get it done" attitude, whatever the task he faces.

To compete at an elite level for most of your life requires a serious amount of mental and physical toughness, and at different times in his life, I think his toughness has come from different sources. He had a rough childhood, and I think at first his toughness came from proving to himself that he had worth as a person. More recently (after the fall) I think his toughness has come from seeing his family, biological and rowing, gather around him and cheer him on. At the end of the day he is down to earth, humble and realistic. He's not a guy for excuses; he just gets the job done. He expects more of himself than anyone around him, and I think that is what is so inspirational.

How bad were things after the accident?
It was bad, really bad. Fighting-for-your-life-in-the-surgical-ICU-hooked-up-to-10-machines-not-being-able-to-communicate-or-even-know-what-was-happening bad. He had rowed almost everyday since he was 15 and was still actively competing and winning at the Masters level when he fell. So a large part of who he is was taken from him in an instant. Processing all of that was/is hard.

Most days now are good days now. I think he actively chooses to not be bitter and to take on this new challenge day by day. But there are still hard days; I would be lying if I said everything was great. I am sure this is by far the hardest mental challenge of his life. We have found laughter really is the best medicine. Dad never took himself too seriously, and our family gatherings always contain a healthy dose of ribbing. Just because he can barely sit up on his own and certainly can't walk doesn't make him immune to the teasing. In fact it makes him an easier target! I think being able to laugh after all this really says something about how tough we humans are.

Will you be pushing him up the steep hills on Thursday?
I absolutely will be. I was not a runner, certainly not the kind who would push 150 lbs up a big hill. I didn't participate in the Thanksgiving Run until Dad's 50th two years ago. I was more interested in staying home and cooking the turkey. But now I feel the same way most runners probably do when they hear someone has been running a race for 51 years in a row–How could you possibly let anything stand in the way of continuing the streak? Dad and I started training recently. (He wasn't discharged from the hospital until July, so we didn't

really get to training until Oct.) I run pushing him, and he helps to propel himself by adding as many strokes as he can, particularly on the hills. By the time we hit the top of some of the hills, my legs and his arms are burning.

How will you feel at the finish on Thursday?
I think we will be very emotional at the finish, especially Dad. Eleven months ago he was lying in a hospital bed with a machine breathing for him, and now he has enough lung power to help propel himself 5.6 miles around a hilly cross country course. It's pretty amazing, all the things that can happen in less than a year. At the finish, I think there might even be some tears.

A History of Boathouse Row

When most organized rowing on the Schuylkill River began, it took place well up river of the current site of Boathouse Row. Before 1822, 1–15 Kelly Drive, Philadelphia, Pennsylvania, just north of the Philadelphia Museum of Art was an industrial area consisting of a series of docks and piers. In 1821 completion of the Fairmount Dam turned a tidal Schuylkill River into a relatively calm, non-tidal, fresh water lake which, when frozen, was ideal for skaters and, when not frozen, became one of the finest rowing venues in the United States. Insightful city officials purchased the forty-five-acre Lemon Hill estate, thirty-three-acre adjacent property and the Sedgeley estate to protect the "spacious basin for boats

against 'the ever-encroaching industry of the expanding city'" (as cited in Beischer, 2006, p. 302–3). Boathouse Row, now a National Historic Landmark, was accepted into the National Register of Historic Places in 1987.

In 1860, the city of Philadelphia, in an attempt to change the architecture of the boathouses to reflect the ideals of moral vigor embodied in rowing, required that all existing clubs demolish their existing buildings and "rebuild in an appropriate style" (Beischer, 2006, p. 300). Not only was the rowing competition between boat clubs fierce but also when rebuilding the structures, the desire for distinction resulted in each boat club's utilization of unique building materials and more intricate irregular structures containing boat storage, dressing rooms, and porches. Early on in the rebuilding process the city and Park Commission enforced many building permit constraints. As time passed and for various reasons, enforcement of these restrictions declined

resulting in the fabrication of vastly different structures in the ensuing 45 years. "Philadelphia's boathouses are more than a mere architectural curiosity, but symbols in built form of late nineteenth-century Philadelphians attempting to distinguish themselves first collectively, and then individually, within a quickly transforming city" (Beischer, p.301).

The Schuylkill Navy, the oldest amateur athletic governing body in the United States, is the governing body that unites the clubs of Boathouse Row. The Schuylkill Navy was formed in 1858 by nine charter members, seven can be confirmed: Camilla, Chebutco, Falcon, Independent, Keystone, Bachelors and Undine

(Stiller, 2005, p. 11). Other clubs that existed around this time and may have been founding members include: Excelsior, Pickwick, Camilla, Philadelphia, Washington, Pennsylvania, Iona (or Ione), Quaker City, Pacific, and Panola. Despite uncertainty surrounding who the founding members were, the original mission is clear, to "secure united action among the several clubs and to promote amateurism on the Schuylkill River" (as cited in Stiller).  When formed, the Schuylkill Navy comprised approximately 300 members. The Schuylkill Navy took on the additional role of keeper-of-the-peace as the surrounding park was sparsely settled and could be dangerous. "Transient men known as 'Schuylkill Rangers' often attacked oarsmen who as a result travelled in bands for protection. The Schuylkill Navy thus served as an informal police force, overseeing the area surrounding the boathouses in addition to enforcing rowing regulations" (as cited in Beischer, 2006, p. 306). Although the duties of the Schuylkill Navy have changed little since its creation, the body it governs has grown. At the 150th Anniversary in 2008 the Schuylkill Navy proudly united 12 boathouses and over 3000 members. The current members include: the University Barge Club (joined 1858), Undine Barge Club (1858), Malta Boat Club (1865), College Boat Club (1875), Vesper Boat Club (1870, resigned 1871, rejoined 1879), Bachelors Barge Club (1859, resigned 1870, rejoined 1882), Fairmount Rowing Association (1916), Penn Athletic Club Rowing Association (1925), Crescent Boat Club (1868), Philadelphia Girls Rowing Club (1967) and Gillin Boat Club (2004).

The Schuylkill Navy resides at #4 Kelly Drive. Originally built by the Pennsylvania Barge Club (PBC) in 1865 by Louis Hickman, the Schuylkill Navy took over the space in 1955. It was at this time when the PBC lost so many members to World War II and the Korean War that it ceased to exist and gave its club to the Schuylkill Navy. In 1974 the building was renamed the "Hollenback House" by the United States Rowing Association, also an occupant, to honor its former president, William M. Hollenback, Jr.

The Schuylkill Navy and its members host a number of events annually. Rowing events include: the Dad Vail Regatta (1953), the Thomas Eakins Head of the

Schuylkill Regatta (1968), the Stotesbury Cup Regatta, and the Philadelphia Frostbite Regatta. The annual cross-county race, the Schuylkill Navy Run, has been held on Thanksgiving morning, since 1899 with a few interruptions during World War II (Stiller, 2005).

The Boathouses

Fairmount Rowing Association
#2 Kelly Drive, (1904) – Founded 1877

Fairmount Rowing Association was formed on September 17, 1877, by a small group of workingmen from the Fairmount neighborhood. They were able to purchase a six-oared barge, which was stored in an old building at Brown and 17th Streets. To row, the members had to carry the boat six blocks to the river. The club was incorporated on October 23, 1880. Fairmount found a permanent home on July 1, 1881, when they took up residence at #2 Boathouse Row, purchasing the building and equipment from Pacific Barge Club. Prior to this, Pacific Barge Club and Quaker City Barge Club owned separate but attached structures, #s 2 and 3, respectively.

In 1904 Fairmount tore down its half of the house and replaced it with a two-and-one half story Georgian Revival brick structure. The architect Walter D. Smedley, a founder of the T-Square Club best known for his residential architecture, was hired. "The Fairmount boathouse, constructed in a distinctly American Georgian Revival style, introduced a design by a well-known architect unlike any other seen on Boathouse Row. Built with three porches, four boat bays, and almost three stories in height, the structure commanded space, and in this way represented the dominance of the Fairmont club, the most feared on the river prior to 1904" (Beischer, 2006, p. 328–9). Of chronological interest is the proximity of Fairmount, the newest structure, to Quaker City, among the oldest. Quaker City was comprised of one small room perched atop of a single boat bay, thus occupying minimum space necessary for boat storage and practice of the sport (Beischer).

Quaker City, organized in 1858 first as Camilla Boat Club, remained in their portion of the building until June 1945. It was then that Fairmount purchased the northern half of the building, a construction project connected the two houses, and the #3 address disappeared.

Fairmount joined the Schuylkill Navy in 1916 and has a long and storied history of successful competition, winning numerous national championships in sweeps and sculls at every level: junior, intermediate, senior, elite, and masters. Among Fairmount's more recent feats, a pair of Fairmount members was recognized as the 2007 Masters Athletes of the Year during the 150th Anniversary celebration of the Schuylkill Navy. Red and Sara Sargent are accomplished scullers in their won right but, in keeping with the standard of 1904, Fairmount continues to dominate and elicit fear in the masters double at the national level.

Crescent Boat Club
#5 Kelly Drive, (1871) – Founded 1867
....

Crescent boat club was organized in 1867, when the Pickwick Barge Club and Iona Barge Club merged membership. At this time they occupied space in what is now Fairmount Rowing Association.

Construction on the first phase of the house occupying #5 happened in conjunction with #4 by Pennsylvania Barge Club. The structure was finished in 1871. It is thought that Charles D. Suplee designed and built the structure. Its main entrance was slightly offset from midline, incorporating stonewalls with brick accents around windows and doors. This design theme was the beginning of a competition between boathouses, which attempted to make the structures more picturesque and more beautiful in their irregularities (Beischer, 2006, p. 314). In 1891 renowned architect Charles Balderston completed the second floor addition. The club colors are red and white.

Crescent joined the Schuylkill Navy in 1868 and incorporated in 1874. Among the club's many victories, one of its earliest may have been one of its finest. It is reported that, in 1872, Crescent won by three-fourths of a length over Undine and West Philadelphia (now Penn AC) boat clubs.

Crescent remained an active and competitive club through the early 1940's. However, because of the declining post-war membership, Crescent turned the operation of the boathouse over to LaSalle College Rowing Association from 1951 to 1960. The house was later reoccupied by Crescent under the leadership of longtime member John Wilkins, which led to the club's rebirth. Others offering significant contributions at that time were Tom Rafferty, Tom and Joe Kealey, Steve Neczypor, Bud Ennis, and Dave Ragan.

Since the 1970's, Crescent has experienced membership growth through novice, junior, and masters programs. In particular, the juniors continue to flourish with many summertime victories and solid representation at the Canadian Henley. Crescent is proud to host the Roman Catholic High School and Merion Mercy Academy rowing programs.

Bachelors Barge Club
#6 Kelly Drive, (1894) – Founded 1853

....

Bachelors Barge Club is the oldest of the 12 existing rowing clubs in the Schuylkill Navy and the oldest continuously operating rowing organization in the United States. Created on June 27, 1853 "to establish a boating club for the cultural benefit and the enjoyment of those concerned," the gilded age of Bachelors Barge athleticism coincided with the Roaring Twenties Legendary

financier Edward T. Stotesbury, who was president of Bachelors from 1927 to 1939. It was around this time that the club produced a plethora of national and Olympic champions lead by such scullers as Kenneth Myers and William Garrett Gilmore. The Depression and World War II hit the Bachelors membership hard. Membership continued to dwindle to an all time low of 10 members in the 1980s. Since then it has experienced a steady resurgence as a place where all are welcome, and instruction is provided for the "cultural benefit and enjoyment of those concerned."

The current boathouse is the fourth structure to house The Bachelors Barge Club. The Club's first home was an 1853 shack on a dock opposite Fairmount Rolling Mills. In 1854 construction began on a brick house that was shared by the

Philadelphia Club. That club disbanded after 1859 and Bachelors became the sole occupant of the boathouse. Bachelors received permission to demolish the brownstone structure in its current location and replace it with a two-story Pompeiian brick building in 1893, becoming the first structure allowed to use brick as its primary building material (Beischer, 2006). Edward Haselhurst and Samuel Huckel, Jr. were the architects hired and, to further distinguish this structure from previous boathouses, incorporated an octagonal pavilion on the second floor above the entrance (Beischer, p. 327). Going one step beyond Malta's Kelly Drive-facing porch, Bachelors built two porches, one over the bay doors with a view of the river and "an arched canopy covered" porch with views of the park creating an opportunity to "display" its prominent members to the public.

In keeping with the founding fathers' vision of a boat club established "for the cultural benefit and the enjoyment of those concerned," Bachelors has an upriver facility, the Button. Built in 1882, the Button served its first dinner on Washington's Birthday 1883 and continues to be the location of the club's annual holiday party.

In addition to the Bachelors rowing programs, the boathouse currently houses the rowing programs for Drexel University and Wharton School of Business Crew. The doors are painted to match their distinctive vertical red and blue striped oar design.

University Barge Club
#7–8 Kelly Drive, (1871) – Founded 1854

There exists controversy over who the University Barge Club (UBC) founders were. Some sources state, on April 25, 1854, ten members of the freshmen class of the University of Pennsylvania formed UBC, while other sources describe the founding fathers as alumni of the University. What is uncontroversial is the influence these your men had on the evolution of collegiate rowing in the United States. Read more about these pioneers in the section describing College Boat Club.

The home of UBC in 1954 is described as a modest wooden structure, used at times as a launching point for the appreciation of "moderate libations" and "moonlit nights." The current building constructed in 1871 replaced a small brick house owned by UBC but occupied by Philadelphia and Washington Boat Clubs (Stiller, 2005). Incorporating Second Empire design, this structure housed  two clubs: University and the now defunct Philadelphia Barge Club (PBC). Echoes of this partnership are clearly visible on the exterior of the house, which has two matching front doors, each with its own address. Numbers 7 and 8, respectively. Inside, the layout is symmetrical, with duplicate stairs to the second floor. The ancient structure is enclosed in the 1893 addition designed by the firm Baker and

Dallet, which demonstrated strong design influence by Frank Furness, the designer of the recently completed Undine boathouse.

"The Lilacs," a farmhouse located on the west bank of the Schuylkill, just upriver of the Strawberry Mansion Bridge, served as a gathering place for social events for half a century. Construction of the Schuylkill Expressway forced the club to abandon The Lilacs in the 1950s. Now the 150 years' worth of pictures and memorabilia occupies PBC's former quarters at #7 and 8 Boathouse Row. Unique to UBC, is the affiliation with Union Boat Club (UBC), in Boston. For more than 60 years, the two clubs have held an annual interclub "UBC" regatta.

University Barge Club boasts 230 members. Having originally been a men's only club, women were admitted as full members in 1990 and a women's locker and shower were built in 1997. Its colors are navy blue and white, recognizable on oars and flags as a three-fold vertical striping dark, light, dark. Since 1964, UBC has been home to the scholastic rowing program of Chestnut Hill Academy and, more recently, to that of its female counterpart, the Springside Academy.

University Barge Club is the organizer and host of the annual Thomas Eakins Head of the Schuylkill Regatta, recently becoming a two-day event due to its popularity. This 2.75 mile headrace had it's beginning in 1968.

Malta Boat Club
#9 Kelly Drive, (1873) – Founded 1860

Members of the Minnehaha Lodge of the Sons of Malta founded Malta Boat Club (then called Malta Barge Club) on February 22, 1860. The character of the club is best described by its symbol, the royal blue Maltese Cross. The four leaves of the cross stand for prudence, justice, temperance and fortitude. Undoubtedly, it was these traits that allowed them to complete their many rowing adventures. In 1860 the club rowed their six-oared barge, the "Minnehaha" down the Delaware to the Chesapeake Bay and up the Elk River. The next year an outing took the men to Port Deposit and Havre de Grace on the Susquehanna. And in 1887 club members rowed a barge from Kensington up the Delaware, through the Raritan Canal, and into New York City, where the New York Athletic Club hosted them. Their fortitude continues to be felt today as evidenced by Malta's consistent national and international presence.

The club initially used a boathouse on Smith's Island in the Delaware River, just off Chestnut Street. In 1863 the club underwent reorganization and moved to the east side of the Schuylkill just above the Spring Garden Street Dam. In 1865 Malta joined the Schuylkill Navy and purchased the clubhouse and boat of the Excelsior Club, which stood on the site of the existing boathouse. Malta absorbed the Keystone Boat club in 1871. Eight years after arriving on the Schuylkill, Malta in conjunction with Vesper Boat Club built semi-attached structures housing the two organizations. Malta's one and one-half story house became too small by 1872, so in 1881 they requested permission to expand. It was at this time that the large Kelly Drive-facing front porch was

built, a trend Bachelors later followed. In 1901, brothers George W. and William D. Hewitt designed substantial additions including a third floor to make Malta the tallest boathouse on Boathouse Row.

The cantilevered portion of the second floor supported by massive diagonal beams over the walkway to the door. This architecture smacks of Undine's design characteristics, as the Hewitts had prior professional ties to Undine's architect, Frank Furness (Beischer, 2006, p. 326). The architectural design continued to follow Undine's example, breaking from tradition by incorporating new materials such as shingles and copper but maintaining the traditional stone, used in this case on the ground floor, "grounding the building in the landscape while referencing the style of earlier boathouses" (Beischer, p. 326).

Vesper Boat Club
#10 Kelly Drive, (1873) – Founded 1865

Anchored by the motto "All Together," Vesper Boat Club has one aim: to develop champions. Producing the first Olympic men's eight gold medal in 1900, Vesper won gold again in 1904 and 1964, the only club in the U.S. to produce three Olympic eight champions.

Founded in 1865 as the Washington Barge Club, Vesper's commitment to winning continues. Each year more than 30 high-caliber athletes train at the recently renovated club.

Other renowned Vesper champions are John B. Kelly, Sr. and later his son, John B. Kelly, Jr. Kelly, Sr. won the Olympic single scull in 1920 and in 1924 with his cousin Paul Costello. But as a laborer, Kelly was barred from entering the Diamond Sculls at the Royal Henley Regatta. Two decades later Kelly, Jr. won that event twice, in 1947 and 1949. Thanks to Jack Kelly, Jr.'s reign and the perpetual high caliber athletes, Vesper holds the record for the most Schuylkill Navy victories and rowing records. At the time of his death, Kelly, Jr. was the president of the U.S. Olympic Committee.

In 1970, after a century of accomplishments, Vesper became the first men's club to organize a women's team. At the 1976 Olympics, six Vesper women rowed in the U.S. women's eight.

The Vesper boathouse was designed by noted Philadelphia architect G. H. Hewitt. The semi-attached ornamental Victorian Gothic architecture is typical of the period, and the Vesper members who were tradesmen constructed the original building with local materials.

College Boat Club
#11 Kelly Drive (1874) – Founded 1872

It is unlikely that the ten University of Pennsylvania freshmen students (or maybe alumni) who founded what became the College Boat Club could have anticipated the impact their actions had on the evolution of collegiate rowing in the United States.

Renting space at Quaker City Barge Club and joining the Schuylkill Navy in 1875, the first important series of intercollegiate races for the young Penn crew included a win at the 1879 Childs Cup and participation in the IRA in 1895. Based on the impressive performances, the crew was invited to Henley Royal Regatta in 1901 — the first of numerous appearances.

Intercollegiate lightweight rowing in the United States began at Penn, with their organization in 1917 of a category for oarsmen weighting 160 pounds or less. From 1919 to 1929, the Penn lightweights suffered just one loss and made their mark. The history of women's rowing at Penn can be traced to 1934, when the sport was offered as a class. In 1967 women's rowing returned as a club sport and since 1975 has enjoyed varsity status. College Boat Club is the only all-collegiate presence on Boathouse Row.

Over the years, the "Quakers" have been home to some of the legendary coaching names in the sport: Joanne Iverson, Barb (Kirsch) Grudt, Joe Wright, Rusty Callows, Joe Burk, Fred Leonard, Ted Nash, and Stan Bergman. The Penn crews, men's and women's lightweight and heavyweight, have posted wins too numerous to mention, making their presence known on both the national and international level.

Originally identified as University Barge Club (UBC) by the ten founding members in 1854, a desire for intercollegiate competition drove the students to separate themselves from UBC and form College Boat Club. In 1874 College Boat Club had amassed enough resources through private subscription to build the current structure occupying #11 Boathouse Row. The two-story brownstone maintained the basic structure of the houses that came before it — Quaker City and Crescent — but with the intent of creating a more beautiful structure, entry into the boathouse was not by way of reception room but by way of the boat bays, introducing a trend subsequent architecture would employ. This distinction was perceived as an improvement in function and style. Constructed in a Victorian Gothic style, an author of an article appearing in an 1876 edition of the University Magazine wrote "The house is all that could be desired by the most exacting, containing all the conveniences and appliances necessary for a complete boat house, and for the comfort of the members. It has the largest boat room on the river and surpasses in its conveniences many of the houses, while in beauty of finish and symmetry of form it is unsurpassed" (as cited in Beischer, 2006, p. 318).

Penn Athletic Club Rowing Association
#12 Kelly Drive (1878)
Founded 1871 (as West Philadelphia Rowing Club)

The first Penn Athletic Club (Penn AC) boat race was a gig race in 1873, and the club celebrated its first victory in the pair at the 1882 Schuylkill Navy Regatta. After this initial victory, Penn AC hasn't stopped winning. Over the ensuing years the club has won more than 168 US Rowing national titles, including the Barnes Trophy, the men's point trophy for the U.S. National Championship, 11 times. On the world stage Penn AC can count 12 world championships wins and nine Olympic medals. In the early 1980's, Ted Nash took over as head coach and accounted for 6 Olympic, 21 world, and 16 Pan-Am medals. In addition six Penn AC members have been Commodores of the Schuylkill Navy: Dr. Robert C. White (1930–34), John B. Kelly, Sr. (1935–41), Jack Bratten (1950), James J. Beckett (1955–56), Joe Sweeney (1985–86), and Vince Dougherty (1988).

The predecessor of Penn AC was West Philadelphia Boat Club, founded in 1871 and located on the west bank of the river near Gray's Ferry Avenue. Its members were largely Irish immigrants, and enjoyed various activities including boating, swimming, and attending plays and dances. They joined the Schuylkill Navy in 1873.

In 1873, when the University of Pennsylvania campus expanded along the lower Schuylkill River, a new boathouse site was located on Boathouse Row, and an ornamental Victorian Gothic Building was erected in 1878. The original request sought permission to "erect an ornamental Brick Boat House" but the request was granted providing stone was used instead of brick, in keeping with established building material requirements (Beischer, 2006, p. 318). Since the West Philadelphia Boat Club could not distinguish itself with building materials, it was built with an L-shaped footprint and an enclosed roof over its second-floor porch, establishing a sense of mysteriousness, being able to look out without being looked upon (Beischer). In 1883 the building was extended to accommodate eight-oar shells. The club name was changed to Penn AC in 1922, when the downtown men's club agreed to sign on as a sponsor. In 1968 an addition was made to accommodate the Saint Joseph's Prep and Monsignor Bonner High School programs.

While Penn AC has a vibrant and decorated past, its mission is firmly rooted in providing future generations of oarsmen and oarswomen with the opportunity to attain their personal best.

Undine Barge Club
#13 Kelly Drive, (1883) – Founded 1856

Undine Barge Club was organized on May 9, 1856, for the intended purpose of "healthful exercise" and "relaxation from business." Named after the spirit of babbling brooks from the Legend of Undine, the club constructed the first of several boathouses, a fifty-foot by eight-foot shed, just a few hundred yards east of the present boathouse. The club purchased a four-oared barge, christened it the "Fawn", and first took it to the water on June 19, 1856. In 1858 Undine and eight other clubs founded The Schuylkill Navy.

The present boathouse was designed by Evans & Furness and built by the

Pennock Brothers in 1882. Taking advantage of the economic decline of the 1870s and the reduced budget of the Park Commission, Undine applied to "replace its single-room structure with a new boathouse," signaling its desire to "exceed the efforts of any previous club both in design and cost, telling the commission, 'we are prepared to expend at least $8,000 in the erection of a new house which in its convenience and adaptability to its purpose and in its architectural appearance will be far in advance of any house in the Park" (Beischer, 2006, p. 321–2). At a cost of $14,000, the building is a splendid example of the architectural genius of Frank Furness, with great beams and trusses, colored cathedral glass windows in the locker room and a carved walnut mantel in the trophy room. Beischer described the design: "the boathouse evoked qualities of its athletes; a fundamental solidity binding the pent-up energy displayed in its combination of tension and compression, presenting the architecture unlike that of earlier boathouses" (p. 325). A two-year historic restoration project was completed in 1998.

While "healthful exercise" was one of the original pursuits of Undine, racing has evolved as the primary focus and interest of Undine's members. A noteworthy race took place on November 18, 1872, when crews from Undine, West Philadelphia (now Penn AC) and Crescent, using boats brought from England, rowed the first eight-oared shell race ever in this country. Undine's rich heritage of rowing success is evident by the numerous trophies and photographs displayed throughout the boathouse and in its upriver clubhouse Castle Ringstetten, designed by Furness and Hewitt and built in 1876.

To complement the profound commitment racing demands and in keeping with the founding fathers' desire for "relaxation from business", the club members regularly share elaborate feasts at their Castle Ringstetten clubhouse. Undine is one of only two clubs that maintains an upriver destination for the express purpose of festive celebrations. Bachelors Barge Club celebrates at their upriver location, The Button.

Philadelphia Girls' Rowing Club
 # 14 Kelly Drive, (1860) – Founded 1938

c. 1870

Philadelphia Girls' Rowing Club (PGRC) is a non-profit corporation duly chartered under the laws of Pennsylvania for the sport of rowing.

The principal purpose of the organization is to promote, stimulate, and support an interest in amateur rowing and other forms of athletics that are supplementary to this sport. On May 4th, 1938 seventeen women, primarily wives of oarsman, founded PGRC. Among them, Ernestine Bayer, considered by some to be "the mother of women's rowing."

The PGRC boathouse actually predates the founding of the club. Built in 1860, making it the oldest building on Boathouse Row, it was constructed as the home of The Philadelphia Skaters' Club and Humane Society, housing skaters in the winter and rowers in the summer. In addition to providing comfort for skaters, the building housed a hospital and an "apparatus used for rescuing persons from a watery grave." There is some controversy as to whether James C. Sidney or Williams S. Andrews designed the structure. It is speculated that they may have worked in tandem. The building contract was awarded to E. Bender and Co. (or Bender and Poulterer) (Stiller, 2005). There is, however, no question about the European-influence on the Italianate style of the structure. Constructed of

semi octagonal-cut greystone, the two-story structure contains a wooden cupola and a river-facing porch extending over three boat bays. The building was complete in spring of 1861 for a total cost of $4,990 (Stiller). Before PGRC took up residence in 1938, University and Undine Barge Clubs had occupied #14, as well as, Quaker City Barge Club and Iona (Ione) and Sedgeley Clubs. Despite it's many tenants over the years, the original building has remained remarkably unaltered (Stiller). The Girls Club purchased the property from the skating club in 1961.

Today the boathouse is wholly owned and operated by women. PGRC is host to the Bill Braxton Memorial Regatta held in November each year. Proceeds from the regatta make it possible to fund scholarships for college freshmen. PGRC is also home to the rowing program of Agnes Irwin Day School for Girls.

PGRC was permitted to join the Schuylkill Navy in the 1960s, and in 1984 Elizabeth Griffin Bergen was elected Commodore of the Schuylkill Navy. In 2008, PGRC proudly celebrated its 70th anniversary.

References

150th Anniversary Schuylkill Navy of Philadelphia, 1858–2008. (2008). Report from 150th Anniversary of the Schuylkill Navy of Philadelphia.

Beischer, T., G. (2006). Controls and Competition: The Architecture of Boathouse Row. The Pennsylvania Magazine of History and Biography, 130(3), 299-329. Retrieved from: http://www.jstor.org/stable/20093871

http://en.wikipedia.org/wiki/Boathouse_Row

http://en.wikipedia.org/wiki/Fairmount_Rowing_Association

http://fairmountrowing.org/

http://maltaboatclub.com/

http://repository.upenn.edu/hp_theses/41

http://tps.cr.nps.gov/nhl/detail.cfm?ResourceId=1985&ResourceType=Building

http://undine.com/wordpress/

http://vesperboatclub.org/wp/

http://www.bachelorsbargeclub.org/

http://www.boathouserow.org/

http://www.crescentboatclub.org/

http://www.livingplaces.com/PA/Philadelphia_County/Philadelphia_City/Boathouse_Row.html

http://www.pennac.org/

http://www.philadelphiagirlsrowingclub.com/home.php

http://www.universitybarge.com/

Stiller, A. (2005). The Philadelphia Girls' Rowing Club: An Incremental Historic Structure Report. Scholarly Commons @ Penn. Retrieved from: http://repository.upenn.edu/hp_theses/41/

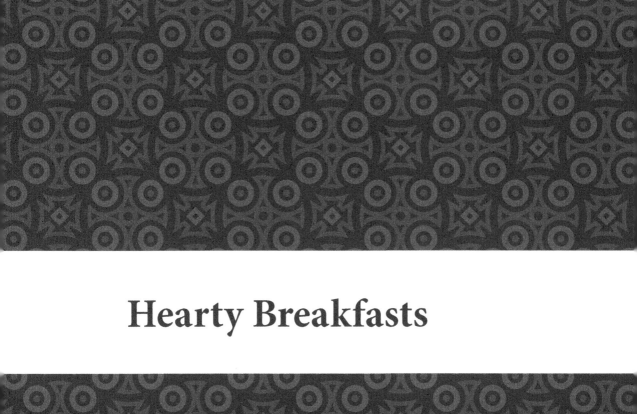

Hearty Breakfasts

Acker Oats

Kate Ackerman – *Cornell University, former national team member and current USRowing team physician.*
Riverside Boat Club | Penn Athletic Club

INGREDIENTS
1 cup oatmeal
1½ cups milk
½ cup All Bran cereal
½ cup raisins
1 tablespoons peanut butter, if I earned it
1 tablespoon Nutella, if I really earned it

DIRECTIONS
1. In a saucepan, cook oatmeal as directed using milk
   in place of water.
2. Add All Bran when oatmeal has 2 minutes left to cook.
3. When oatmeal is cooked, stir in raisins, peanut butter and Nutella. Enjoy!

Orange Juice Pancakes

Bachelors Barge Club

INGREDIENTS

2 cups flour
1 teaspoons salt
2 teaspoons baking soda
¼ cup sugar
1¾ cups orange juice
¼ cup butter, melted
Vanilla yogurt
Pecans
Butter or oil for griddle

DIRECTIONS

1. In a medium bowl, mix dry ingredients together.
2. In a small bowl, beat eggs, and then add orange juice and melted butter. Mix well and add to dry ingredients.
3. On a hot, oiled griddle, spoon on batter. When bubbles form on the surface, flip. Cook until brown on both sides. Serve topped with vanilla yogurt and pecans.

Makes 8 pancakes.

Lightweight Pancake

Kate Sauks *won the Head of the Charles lightweight four in 2009 and is a dynamite duo with her lightweight sister winning Ontario University Rowing Championships in 2010 and Row Ontario Championships in 2011.*
Hanlan Boat Club

INGREDIENTS
2 teaspoons canola oil, for griddle
2 eggs
½ to ¾ cup oatmeal
Sprinkle of frozen fruit, blueberries or raspberries
Sprinkle of cinnamon
Topping suggestions:
Cream cheese
Peanut or almond butter

DIRECTIONS
1. Preheat griddle on medium heat, add oil.
2. In a small bowl, beat eggs. Stir in oatmeal, and cinnamon and frozen fruit if desired.
3. Pour mixture onto griddle and cook until underside is brown (approximately 3 minutes), then flip and continue cooking until cooked through.
4. Eat warm with toppings of choice, or let cool and make into a sandwich as a healthy alternative to bread for lunch or snack!

Makes 1 giant pancake.

Susan's Breakfast Casserole

Malta Boat Club

INGREDIENTS

6 slices white bread, crust removed and cubed
1 large onion, chopped
2 tablespoons butter
1–2 cups ham, cubed or cooked breakfast sausage
8 eggs, beaten
3 cups milk
½ teaspoon dry mustard
½ teaspoon garlic powder
Dash of salt and pepper
2–3 cups cheese (Swiss or Cheddar), grated

DIRECTIONS

1. Grease bottom of 9 × 13 inch casserole dish. Place bread cubes in prepared pan.
2. In a frying pan, sauté onion in butter until translucent. Pour onion and butter mixture over bread. Sprinkle ham or sausage over bread and onion.
3. In a medium bowl, mix eggs, milk, mustard, garlic, salt and pepper. Pour egg mixture on top of bread. Top with grated cheese. Cover with plastic wrap and chill in refrigerator overnight.
4. Preheat oven to 250° F. Bake for about 30 minutes until bubbling and golden brown.

Serves 6.

Head of the Schuylkill Volunteer Breakfast Egg Strata

Margaret Meigs
University Barge Club

INGREDIENTS
9 slices sandwich bread, cubed
1½ tablespoons onion, chopped (optional)
½ pound Cheddar cheese, grated
6 eggs
3 cups milk
1 teaspoon Worcestershire sauce
1 teaspoon dry mustard
½ teaspoon salt
½ teaspoon pepper
Optional additions include any one of the following:
½ pound bacon, cooked crisp, crumbled
½ pound sausage, cooked and drained
1 cup sliced mushrooms, sautéed

DIRECTIONS
1. In a 2-quart, buttered baking dish, layer the bread, onion and cheese. Optional ingredients should be layered now.
2. In a mixing bowl, beat eggs, milk, Worcestershire sauce, mustard, salt and pepper together and pour over the layered ingredients. Cover, put in the refrigerator overnight.
3. In the morning bake for 1 hour at 325° F or until puffed and the center is set.

Serves 8.

Rita's Pancake Non Pareil

INGREDIENTS
½ cup flour
½ cup milk
2 eggs, slightly beaten
Pinch of nutmeg
4 tablespoons butter, melted in 12 inch skillet with heatproof handle
2 tablespoons confectioners' sugar
Juice of ½ lemon

DIRECTIONS
1. Preheat oven to 425° F.
2. In a medium bowl, combine flour, milk, eggs and nutmeg. Beat lightly. Leave batter a little lumpy.
3. Melt butter in a 12 inch skillet with heatproof handle. When pan is very hot, pour in batter.
4. Bake in oven 15–20 minutes until golden brown. Remove from oven and sprinkle with sugar, return briefly to oven.
5. Remove from oven and sprinkle with lemon juice. Serve with jelly, jam or marmalade.

Makes 1 pan.

On-The-Go

Breakfast Bars

Kris Benarcik
Wilmington Rowing Center

INGREDIENTS

1 14-ounce can condensed milk
2 ½ cups rolled oats, not instant
1 cup coconut, shredded
1 cup dried cranberries
1 cup mixed seeds (pumpkin, sunflower, sesame)
1 cup natural unsalted peanuts
Canola oil for greasing pan and hands

DIRECTIONS

1. Preheat the oven to 250° F and grease a 9 × 13 inch baking pan.
2. Warm the condensed milk over low heat but do not boil.
3. In a large bowl, combine oats, coconut, cranberries, seeds and peanuts. Add the warmed condensed milk and use a rubber spatula to gently mix.
4. Spread the mixture into the oiled pan and press down with a spatula (or your clean oiled hands) to make the surface even.
5. Bake for one hour. Remove and let cool for 10–15 minutes then cut into squares. Let cool completely. Store in an airtight container.

Makes 16 bars.

Energy Candy Bar

Jane Toro
Berkeley Paddling and Rowing Club

INGREDIENTS
1 15-ounce can sweetened condensed milk
2 cups of dry milk powder, more if needed
¼ cup of raisins or other dried fruit
¼ cup of chopped nuts

DIRECTIONS
1. Mix the dry milk powder into the condensed milk, add raisins, and nuts until it is like very stiff cookie dough.
2. Press mixture into a greased 9 × 9 inch pan and refrigerate. It will be the consistency of fudge when it cools. Cut into little squares. This is very rich and sweet so a little goes a long way.

Makes 1 pan.

This recipe lends itself to a lot of variations with additions of any of the following: peanut butter, chocolate chips or cocoa, granola, maple syrup, almond flavoring...

My track coach, Ken Simmons, gave the recipe to all the moms to make for their young athletes. Mr. Simmons is 102 now and there is an invitational named after him at the University of Michigan where he was the coach of the first varsity women's track team.

Raw Date Energy Bars *by Moira Nordholt, The Feel Good Guru*

Jane Toro
Berkeley Paddling and Rowing Club

INGREDIENTS
1 cup fresh or dried dates, pitted
1½ cups organic almonds
1 banana
½ cup cacao nibs
1 teaspoon vanilla extract
Dried shredded coconut

DIRECTIONS
1. If using dried dates, soak them for a few minutes in just enough water or orange juice to cover, then drain.
2. Pulse the almonds in a dry food processor until they're broken up but still in crunchy chunks. Add the banana, cocoa nibs, vanilla and dates and blend just until mixed.
3. Sprinkle ½ the coconut on the bottom of a 9 × 9 inch baking pan. Scrape the nut mixture onto the pan and spread it out evenly, pressing down gently with your hands. Sprinkle rest of coconut over the top.
4. Placing pan in the refrigerator for an hour or more will make the bars easier to cut and serve, but these are at their gooey, datey, tasty best at room temperature.

Makes 1 pan.

The Lightweight Canoe

Vesper Boat Club

INGREDIENTS
1 Power Bar — any flavor you prefer
¼–½ cup Fiber One cereal

DIRECTIONS
This is pretty much the standard lightweight meal.
1. Take the Power Bar and put it in your pocket for about 10 minutes to soften it up.
2. Remove Power Bar from pocket and unwrap completely. Take Power Bar and upturn the sides to create a "canoe-like" shape.
3. Fill the canoe with Fiber One pellets and enjoy!

Makes 1 bar.

Appetizers

Feta and Sun Dried Tomato Torta

Mimi Hanks-Bell – *I am new to rowing but not to the kitchen. Fortunately for my family and friends I am a better cook than a rower.*
Bachelors Barge Club

INGREDIENTS
¼ cup pine nuts
1 medium clove garlic, peeled
1 small shallot, peeled
¼ pound unsalted butter, cut into pieces, at room temperature
12 ounces feta cheese, cut into pieces, at room temperature
1 8-ounce package light cream cheese, cut into pieces, at room temperature
¼ teaspoon Tabasco sauce
1 3-ounce jar sun dried tomatoes packed in oil, drained, cut into small pieces with scissors
6 ounces pesto

DIRECTIONS
1. Toast pine nuts in a dry skillet over medium heat until golden. Watch carefully to prevent burning. Remove from skillet, set aside.
2. Turn on food processor, with machine running drop garlic and shallot through the feed tube. Chop finely.
3. While food processor is running, add butter, feta, cream cheese and Tabasco sauce. Process until smooth and blended.
4. Oil a 4 to 5 cup mold, bowl or container; line with a piece of plastic wrap long enough to fold over top when filled. Spread with half of pesto, sprinkle with half of tomatoes and half of pine nuts. Next, layer all the cheese mixture followed by the remaining pesto, tomatoes and pine nuts. Fold plastic wrap over top and refrigerate overnight.
5. About one hour before serving, remove the torta from refrigerator. Fold plastic wrap back and unmold onto a serving platter. Surround with crackers or cut vegetables.

Serves 20.

Ginny's Phenomenal Bean Dip

Ginny Kaufmann *who drank more beer than any other female oarswoman in the late 70's and early 80's!*
Vesper Boat Club

INGREDIENTS
1 can black beans
1 can red beans
1 can whole kernel corn
1 large jar hot salsa

DIRECTIONS
In a large bowl, combine all ingredients and mix well. Serve with tortilla chips. Enjoy!

Serves 8–10.

Ginny's Phenomenal Artichoke Dip

Ginny Kaufmann
Vesper Boat Club

INGREDIENTS
1 large can marinated artichoke hearts, drained, chopped
1 cup mayonnaise
1 cup Parmesan cheese

DIRECTIONS
Preheat oven to 350° F.
1. In a medium bowl, combine all ingredients and mix well.
2. Place mixture in ovenproof dish.
3. Bake for 20 minutes, until top is golden brown
   (in spots).
4. Serve with either Wheat Thins or Triscuits. Enjoy!

Serves 8–10.

Dill Dip

Alison Simmons *is a junior rower who enjoys rowing!*
Steel City Rowing Club

INGREDIENTS
1 cup sour cream
1 cup mayonnaise
1 tablespoon dried onion, diced
1 tablespoon dried dill

DIRECTIONS
1. In a medium bowl, mix all four ingredients.
2. Cover and chill in refrigerator for at least 3 hours.
3. Serve with crackers or vegetables.

Makes 2 cups of dip.

Avocado Black Bean Dip

Brandon & Linda Eck
Malta Boat Club

INGREDIENTS

2 avocados, sliced and chopped into small cubes
Juice of 2–3 limes
1 15-ounce can black beans, drained and rinsed
1 15-ounce can whole kernel corn (white), drained
1 Jalapeño pepper, seeded and chopped
2 Serrano peppers, seeded and chopped
⅓ cup red onion, finely chopped
½ teaspoon salt
½ teaspoon ground cumin
¼ teaspoon cayenne pepper

DIRECTIONS

1. In a medium bowl, pour 3 tablespoons of lime juice over avocado cubes to keep avocado from browning. Add beans, corn, peppers and onion. Add spices and more lime juice.
2. Stir gently. Adjust seasoning with salt and more lime juice.

Serves 10.

Artichoke-Asparagus Wonton Twists

Susan Butterweck *learned to scull at a Schuylkill River Development Committee-sponsored Learn to Row program in the summer of 1999, joined Bachelors shortly after, and has been rowing, sometimes competing, on the Schuylkill since.*
Bachelors Barge Club

INGREDIENTS
1 small bunch asparagus, cut into 1 inch pieces
1 cup frozen artichoke hearts
1 12-ounce package 3 × 3 inch wonton wrappers
4 ounces goat cheese
4 ounces Havarti with dill, shredded
1–2 tablespoon plain yogurt
¼ cup fresh dill
Salt and pepper
1 egg

DIRECTIONS
1. Boil asparagus until very tender, set aside to cool.
2. Thaw artichoke hearts.
3. In a food processor or blender, add goat cheese and yogurt, blend to soften. Continue processing while adding dill and shredded Havarti. Add cooled asparagus and artichokes, process until smooth.
4. In a small dish, whisk egg with one tablespoon of water.
5. Prepare baking sheet(s) with a silicon baking liner or sheet of parchment. Brush one side of wonton wrapper with egg, lay egg side down on baking sheet and brush corners of other side with egg mixture. Place approximately ½ teaspoon of cheese-vegetable filing in the center of the wrapper. Pinch corners together above the filling.
6. Bake at 375° F for 10 minutes or until wanton edges are golden brown. Serve warm.

Makes 48 pieces.

Breads and Rolls

Banana Bread

Maria Dreher
Malta Boat Club

INGREDIENTS
1 cup sugar
½ cup (1 stick) butter
1 teaspoon baking soda
1 tablespoon orange juice
2 eggs, well beaten
3 ripe bananas, mashed
2 cups flour
¼ cup chopped nuts (optional)
¼ cup chocolate ships (optional)

DIRECTIONS
1. Preheat oven to 350° F.
2. Butter or spray the sides and bottom of a loaf pan.
3. In a very small bowl combine baking soda and orange juice.
4. In a medium mixing bowl, cream together butter and sugar. Add eggs, bananas, soda and juice mixture, and flour, mixing thoroughly. Stir in nuts and or chocolate chips if desired.
5. Bake for 1 hour. Cool before slicing.

Makes 1 loaf.

Navajo Fry Bread

Malta Boat Club

INGREDIENTS
2 cups flour
2 teaspoons baking powder
½ teaspoon salt
½ cup powdered milk
Warm water
2–3 cups canola oil or shortening for frying
½ cup powdered sugar or honey (optional)

DIRECTIONS
1. In a large bowl, mix together flour, baking powder, salt and powdered milk. Stir in enough warm water until dough just clings together.
2. On a floured countertop, knead the dough until it is soft, not sticky. Cover with a cloth and let stand for 2 hours.
3. Shape into 12 balls about 2–3 inches across. Flatten each ball by patting with hands until dough forms a circle about 8 inches in diameter. Make a hole in the center.
4. Fry in about ½ inch of oil or shortening. Bread should be light brown on each side. Use tongs to turn. Drain on paper towels. Top with powdered sugar or honey.

Makes 12 fry breads.

Salads

Easy, Delicious Salad Dressing

Margaret Meigs
University Barge Club

INGREDIENTS
¼ cup red wine vinegar or — even better — white balsamic vinegar
¾ cup olive oil
⅓ cup chopped shallots
½ teaspoon salt
½ teaspoon black pepper
½ teaspoon sugar

DIRECTIONS
1. Mix all ingredients except for the olive oil in a small bowl.
2. Whisk in the olive oil. Will dress several small salads. Leftover dressing will keep well in a jar in the refrigerator.

Ginny's Phenomenal Pizza Salad

Ginny Kaufmann *who drank more beer than any other female oarswoman in the late 70's and early 80's!*
Vesper Boat Club

INGREDIENTS

1 pound bag wagon wheel pasta, cooked al dente and drained
2 large tomatoes, chopped
1 green pepper, seeded, chopped
1 onion, chopped
8 ounces pepperoni, chopped
4–8 ounces Parmesan cheese
1 bottle Italian salad dressing

DIRECTIONS

In a large bowl, combine all ingredients and mix well. Enjoy! This is great for a hot day picnic because there is no mayo.

Serves 8–10.

Fiesta Salad

Ellen Strom
Wilmington Rowing Center

INGREDIENTS

1 10-ounce package blend of romaine and leaf lettuce
1 15-ounce can black beans, rinsed and drained well
1 pint grape or cherry tomatoes, halved
1 10-ounce package of frozen corn kernels, thawed
¾ cup radishes, thinly sliced
½ cup small red onion, peeled and sliced
1 ripe avocado, chopped
1 cup chopped red bell pepper
½ cup crumbled feta cheese, additional feta for topping.
Honey-Lime Dressing:
¼ cup fresh lime juice
½ cup canola oil
¼ cup red wine vinegar
2 tablespoon honey
2 tablespoon fresh cilantro, finely chopped
2 teaspoon garlic, minced

DIRECTIONS

1. In a small bowl, mix all Honey-Lime Dressing ingredients until combined.
2. In a large bowl, toss all salad ingredients just before serving.
3. Pour most of dressing over salad; toss until evenly distributed. Reserve some dressing for serving.
4. Season to taste with salt & freshly ground black pepper.
5. Serve immediately with additional cheese and Honey-Lime dressing on the side.

Serves 8–10.

New Potato and Green Bean Salad

Marie Cooney
Vesper Boat Club

INGREDIENTS
¼ cup balsamic vinegar
2 tablespoon Dijon mustard
2 tablespoon fresh lemon juice
1 or 2 garlic cloves, minced
Dash of Worcestershire sauce
½ cup extra-virgin olive oil
Salad:
1½ pounds small new potatoes, quartered
¾ pound haricot verts, or other green beans, cut in half
1 small red onion, coarsely chopped
¼ cup fresh basil, chopped

DIRECTIONS
1. In a medium bowl, whisk together vinegar, mustard, lemon juice, garlic and Worcestershire sauce. Gradually whisk in oil. Season to taste with salt and pepper.
2. In a large saucepan, add potatoes with enough water to cover them. Cook until nearly tender, about 8 minutes. Add green beans and cook 2 more minutes. Drain potatoes and beans. Immerse in ice water to cool.
3. Combine green beans, potatoes, onion and basil in large bowl. Add dressing, toss to coat.

Can be made 4 hours ahead. Let stand at room temperature before serving.

Serves 6.

Corn and Red Onion Salad

Bachelors Barge Club

INGREDIENTS
5 ears corn, shucked
1 red onion, cut in half inch slices
1 green pepper, quartered lengthwise
1 red pepper, quartered lengthwise
2 Jalapeños (optional)
½ cup low-fat sour cream
2 tablespoon lime juice
1 small bunch cilantro
½ teaspoon kosher salt
1 avocado, sliced
1 head butter lettuce, washed and dried

DIRECTIONS
1. Grill or broil corn, onion, peppers and jalapeños over a hot grill until lightly charred, turning once. When cool enough to handle, cut the corn from the cobs, chop the onion and peppers, and remove the stem and seeds from the jalapeños.
2. Purée the jalapeños with the sour cream, lime juice, cilantro, and salt until smooth in a food processor. Pour over the corn, onion, peppers and avocado mixture and toss to coat. Serve on the lettuce.

Serves 6.

Lentil Salad

Izzie Brown
Northfield Mount Hermon | Rollins College
Bachelors Barge Club | Berkeley Paddling and Rowing Club

INGREDIENTS

2 cups French or green lentils, rinsed, cleaned and picked over
2 carrots, peeled and diced
2 cloves garlic, smashed
1 bay leaf
2 cups shelled edamame
1 shallot, minced
2 tablespoons Dijon mustard
3 tablespoons red wine vinegar
1 teaspoon kosher salt
1 teaspoon honey
⅓ cup extra-virgin olive oil
Freshly ground black pepper
1 head butter or Boston lettuce

DIRECTIONS

1. In a medium pot, add enough water to cover the lentils, carrots, garlic and bay leaf by 1 inch. Bring to a boil. Reduce heat and simmer, partially covered, until the lentils are just tender, 12–20 minutes. Toss in the edamame. Drain and discard the bay leaf.
2. In a large bowl, make the dressing by whisking together the shallot, mustard, vinegar, honey and salt. Slowly add the oil, continuing to whisk. Toss the lentils with the dressing and season with pepper.
3. Arrange the lettuce on a large platter or individual plates. Spoon the warm lentils over the lettuce.

Serves 6.

Black-Eyed Johnny Salad

Bachelors Barge Club

INGREDIENTS
1 16-ounce package of black-eyed peas
1 carrot, grated
1 red onion, minced
1½ cups whole kernel corn, cooked
1 red bell pepper, finely chopped
5 stalks of celery, finely chopped
1 bunch fresh dill, chopped
Dressing:
2 cups white wine vinegar
2 cups olive oil
3 tablespoons sugar
1 tablespoons salt
1 teaspoon pepper
1½ teaspoon garlic, minced

DIRECTIONS
1. Cook black-eyed peas in a large pot of water until al dente, about 15–20 minutes. Drain and cool.
2. In a large bowl, combine carrot, onion, corn, pepper, celery, dill and peas.
3. In a small bowl, whisk together vinegar, oil, sugar, salt, pepper and garlic.
4. Pour dressing over vegetable and peas mixture.

Serves 8.

Vegetables and Side Dishes

Windsor Grilled Veggies

Mr. & Mrs. Windsor – *Mail Carrier for Boathouse Row*

INGREDIENTS

Choose any of your favorite raw vegetables. Here are my favorites:
2 cups Broccoli florets
2 cups Cauliflower
2 cups Brussels sprouts, each cut in half
2 cups Sweet potatoes, peeled and cut in small chunks
2 cups Whole mushrooms, cut in half
1–2 fresh corn on cob, husked, cut into 3 pieces per ear
⅓ cup olive oil
2 tablespoons garlic powder
2 tablespoons onion powder
1 cup fresh basil, cut up
½ cup Parmesan cheese
1 tablespoon pepper
Couple of full squirts Liquid Braggs OR 1 tablespoon sea salt
2–3 tablespoons sweet chili sauce

DIRECTIONS

1. Preheat oven to 500° F.
2. Clean and cut all of the vegetables into bite size pieces. Arrange in a large enough pan to get vegetables into one layer. Try to get vegetables on one layer. If they overlap, plan on turning them during cooking.
3. Douse veggies with olive oil. Sprinkle garlic powder, onion powder and fresh basil. Liquid or sea salt and pepper to taste.
4. Place in oven uncovered until veggies are browned on edges, approximately 20 minutes.
5. When vegetables are done brush on chili sauce for a spicy, sweet kick; Shoprite has their own brand that is awesome. Lastly, sprinkle with Parmesan cheese and enjoy!

Serves 4–5.

Sid's Roasted Corn

Cheryl Cook & Barbara Spitz
University Barge Club

INGREDIENTS
6 ears of corn, shucked
2–3 tablespoons olive oil
Kosher salt
Freshly ground pepper
1 lime

DIRECTIONS
1. Preheat oven to 375° F.
2. Pour olive oil into bottom of baking dish large enough to hold all ears in a row. Roll 3 ears of corn in oil to coat. Repeat with next 3 ears. Place all 6 ears in dish. Sprinkle with salt and pepper. Roll to coat.
3. Bake in oven for 30–40 minutes. Turn occasionally when bottom of ears start to caramelize. Serve with a wedge of lime. Enjoy.

Serves 6.

Autumn Roasted Vegetables

Malta Boat Club

INGREDIENTS
1 acorn squash, butternut squash or small pumpkin, chopped into 1 inch chunks
2 green apples, chopped
1 cup fresh cranberries
1 tablespoon canola oil

DIRECTIONS
1. Preheat oven to 400° F.
2. Chop squash and apple. Put on roasting pan with oil and bake for 45 minutes.
3. Remove from oven, add berries and return to oven for 15 more minutes.

Serves 6.

Chinese Green Beans

Bachelors Barge Club

INGREDIENTS

1 pound green beans, washed, ends trimmed
3 tablespoons vegetable or peanut oil for stir-frying
1 tablespoon garlic, chopped
1 tablespoon ginger, chopped
1 tablespoon dark soy sauce
2 teaspoons Chinese rice wine or dry sherry
1½ teaspoons corn starch
3 tablespoons broth

DIRECTIONS

1. Prepare sauce: in small dish combine soy sauce, Chinese rice wine, corn starch and broth. Set aside.
2. Heat oil in wok or large frying pan on medium high. When oil is hot, add garlic and ginger. Cook for one minute. Add beans and stir-fry until the skins of the beans pucker and turn brown and the beans are not quite tender, 5–7 minutes. While the beans are still cooking, stir sauce and pour over beans. Cook 2 more minutes.

Serves 4.

The One Way I Will Actually Eat Brussels Sprouts

Karen Lewis
Vesper Boat Club | Philadelphia Adaptive Rowing

INGREDIENTS
1 bag Brussels sprouts
10 strips of the most fabulous bacon you can find

DIRECTIONS
1. Preheat oven to 350° F.
2. Cut Brussels sprouts in half.
3. Place bacon strips on the bottom of a 9 × 9 inch baking pan and fill pan with halved Brussels sprouts. Top with the rest of the bacon strips.
4. Place in oven for 50 minutes. Yum!

Serves 6.

Baked Corn Casserole

Malta Boat Club

INGREDIENTS

1 can creamed corn
1 can whole kernel corn
1 8.5 ounce box Jiffy cornbread mix
1 stick butter, melted
1 cup sour cream
2 eggs, beaten

DIRECTIONS

1. Preheat oven to 350° F.
2. In a large bowl, mix all ingredients together until smooth. Pour into a 2 quart baking dish.
2. Cook in oven for 45 minutes.

Serves 8.

Delicious Squash Casserole

Malta Boat Club

INGREDIENTS
3 pounds smooth yellow squash
1–2 onions, diced finely
3 carrots, shredded
½ can cream of chicken soup
1 small jar pimentos
½ pint sour cream
1 bag Pepperidge Farm herbed stuffing, reserve ½ cup for topping
1 cup butter, melted or canola oil

DIRECTIONS
1. Preheat oven to 350° F.
2. Line the bottom of a 9 × 13 inch pan with the stuffing mix; pour the melted butter (or oil) over it.
2. Peel squash and boil until tender. In a large mixing bowl, mash coarsely; drain well. Add onions, carrots, chicken soup, pimentos and sour cream. Mix well and pour into pan. Sprinkle the remaining stuffing mix on top.
3. Bake uncovered for 20 minutes.

Serves 8.

Baked Pineapple

Malta Boat Club

INGREDIENTS

1 stick butter, melted or ½ cup canola oil
4 slices bread, cubed
2 large eggs, beaten
½ cup sugar
1 20-ounce can crushed pineapple with juice
1 tablespoon flour
A dash of salt or so to taste

DIRECTIONS

1. Preheat oven to 350° F.
2. In a large mixing bowl, combine butter, bread, eggs, sugar, pineapple, and flour. Pour into casserole dish.
3. Bake for 30–40 minutes.

Serves 6.

Pineapple Stuffing

Malta Boat Club

INGREDIENTS

2 20-ounce cans crushed pineapple, drained
13 pieces white bread, cubed
3 eggs, beaten
⅔ cup sugar
3 tablespoons flour
¼ cup butter, melted

DIRECTIONS

1. Preheat oven to 325° F.
2. In a large mixing bowl, combine all ingredients and blend well.
3. Bake uncovered in casserole dish for 1 hour.

Serves 10.

Juliana Salad

Juliana Griffin
Bachelors Barge Club | Berkeley Paddling and Rowing Club

INGREDIENTS

½ package Trader Joe's Harvest Grains Blend, or other grain mix
2 cups water or broth
⅓ cup olive oil
2 tablespoon lemon juice
2 tablespoon balsamic vinegar
Kosher salt and freshly ground pepper to taste
2 cups any raw vegetables & herbs, chopped
Suggestions:
½ cup carrots, chopped
½ cup celery, chopped
½ cup peppers, chopped
½ cup frozen peas or corn, thawed
¼ cup parsley, basil or cilantro, chopped
¼ cup red onion, minced

DIRECTIONS

1. Cook grain mix as directed in water or broth. Remove from heat and set aside.
2. While grains are cooking, in a medium bowl combine olive oil, lemon juice, vinegar, vegetables and herbs.
3. Pour warm grains over vegetable mixture. Salt and pepper to taste and serve warm.

Serves 6.

Easy Cole Slaw

Malta Boat Club

INGREDIENTS
1 package cole slaw mix
2 tablespoons white vinegar
2 tablespoons milk
1 teaspoon sugar
½ cup mayonnaise
½ cup onion, finely chopped (optional)
½ cup carrots, shredded (optional)

DIRECTIONS
In a large mixing bowl, combine vinegar, milk, sugar and mayonnaise, mixing well. Add cole slaw and optional vegetables.

Serves 8.

Soups and Stews

White Bean and Kale Soup

Kris Benarcik
Wilmington Rowing Center

INGREDIENTS

2 medium onions, chopped
2 tablespoons olive oil
5 garlic cloves, smashed
½ teaspoon dried oregano, crumbled
5 cups low-sodium chicken broth (40 fluid ounces)
1 pound kale, cut into 2 inch pieces (16 cups)
1 16 to 19-ounce can white beans, rinsed and drained
Accompaniments:
Grated Parmigiano-Reggiano; extra-virgin olive oil, crusty bread

DIRECTIONS

1. In a large heavy pot over moderate heat, cook onions in oil stirring occasionally, until softened, about 5 minutes. Add garlic and oregano and cook, stirring frequently, 2 minutes.
2. Stir in broth and bring to a boil. Stir in kale and beans, then simmer, uncovered, until kale is tender, about 15 minutes.
3. Transfer 2 cups of soup to a blender and purée until smooth (use caution when blending hot liquids), and then stir into remaining soup to thicken. Season with salt and pepper. Serve sprinkled with cheese and drizzled with oil.

Serves 8–10.

This is even better if made a day ahead and reheated.

Pennsylvania Dutch Chicken Corn Soup

Theresa A. Savard – *Theresa has been an active member of PGRC since 1972 and rowed for Cambridge Boat Club in college. She and Ted Trocky of Malta Boat Club had great success at Masters Nationals.*
Philadelphia Girls Rowing Club

INGREDIENTS

4 to 4½ pound soup chicken
2 medium size onions, quartered
2 medium size carrots, chopped
2 stalks of celery, chopped
1 bay leaf
Lots of parsley
Salt & pepper to taste
2 chicken bouillon cubes
8 cups water
6–7 hard-boiled eggs
3–4 cups of fresh corn
1 cup of cooked rice

DIRECTIONS

1. In a large Dutch oven place chicken, onions, carrots, celery, bay leaf and parsley and bring to a boil. Cover and simmer about 2½ hours.
2. Meanwhile cook the rice.
3. Remove chicken from broth to cool. Pour broth through a sieve and discard vegetables. Cube or shred chicken and re-combine with broth along with rice, corn and chopped eggs. Add salt and pepper to taste.

Serves 8–10.

West African Peanut Soup

Andrea Greeley
University of Rhode Island | Bachelors Barge Club

INGREDIENTS

2 cups onion, chopped
1 tablespoon oil
½ teaspoon cayenne pepper
1 teaspoon peeled fresh ginger, grated
1 cup carrots, chopped
2 cups sweet potatoes, chopped
4 cups vegetable stock or water
2 cups tomato juice
1 cup smooth peanut butter
1 tablespoon sugar (optional)
1 cup scallions or chives, chopped

DIRECTIONS

1. In a stockpot, sauté onions in oil. Stir in cayenne and ginger. Add carrots and sauté a couple more minutes. Mix in sweet potatoes and stock or water. Bring to a boil, reduce heat and simmer for about 15 minutes, when vegetables are tender.
2. Use a handheld blender or a food processor to purée the vegetables and liquid. Add tomato juice and peanut butter, stir until smooth. If desired, add sugar. Garnish with scallions or chives.

Serves 6.

Chicken & Winter Vegetable Soup

Malta Boat Club

INGREDIENTS

2 tablespoons butter
2 large onions, chopped
1 teaspoon garlic, chopped
1 pound skinless boneless chicken, chopped
¾ pound peeled potatoes, chopped
¼ pound peeled turnips, chopped
¼ pound carrots, peeled and chopped
5 cups chicken broth
½ teaspoon thyme
1 bay leaf

DIRECTIONS

1. In a stockpot, melt butter. Add onion and garlic, sauté for 5 minutes. Add chicken and brown. Add potatoes, turnips and carrots and sauté for 10 minutes.
2. Add chicken broth, thyme and bay leaf and bring to a boil. Reduce heat to low and simmer for 30 minutes or until vegetables are tender.

Serves 6.

Lentil Soup Madrilena

INGREDIENTS
1 large onion, chopped
1 green pepper, diced
4 tablespoons canola oil
2 tablespoons flour
1 16-ounce can tomatoes (or 2 fresh tomatoes)
4 large carrots, diced
2 tablespoons salt
1 pound lentils, washed and picked over
2 quarts water

DIRECTIONS
1. In a stockpot, sauté onion and pepper in oil. Stir in flour and cook gently just until bubbly. Don't brown.
2. Add all remaining ingredients. Cook covered over very low heat for 2 hours. Stirring occasionally (it may stick because of the flour).

Serves 12.

Keeps very well. Add a little water when reheating.

Beef Goulash

Janet and Ted Nash
Penn Athletic Club

INGREDIENTS

1 ½ pounds boneless lean beef chuck or beef stew meat, cut into 1 ½ inch cubes
⅓ cup oil
2 medium onions, chopped
2 tablespoons flour
½ to ¾ teaspoon salt, to taste
1 tablespoon paprika
Dash thyme
1 pound can whole tomatoes (2 cups)
8-ounce can seasoned tomato sauce
3 beef bullion cubes
1 glove garlic, minced
1 bouquet garni (bay leaf, celery stalk, parsley sprig tied together)
1 package egg noodles

DIRECTIONS

1. In a pan, brown beef slowly in hot oil to develop flavor. Add onions and cook until onions are tender. Stir in flour, salt, paprika, and thyme.
2. Drain tomatoes, reserving liquid. Add water to liquid to make 1 ½ cups and add to meat. Add tomatoes and remaining ingredients to meat mixture, heat to boiling.
3. Reduce heat, cover and simmer, do not boil, for about 1½ hours or until meat is tender, stirring occasionally. Remove bouquet garni. Serve with hot noodles.

Serves 6.

Brazilian Seafood Stew

Malta Boat Club

INGREDIENTS

1 tablespoon olive oil
1 medium onion, chopped
1 red, yellow and green bell pepper, chopped
2 plum tomatoes, chopped
2 Serrano chilies, seeded and minced
2 teaspoons salt
1 teaspoon pepper
3 cups fish stock
½ can low-fat coconut milk
6 scallions
1 pound white fish
1 pound shrimp
Juice of one lime
⅓ cup cilantro, chopped

DIRECTIONS

1. In a medium stockpot, over medium-high heat, add oil, sauté onion and bell peppers for 5 minutes.
   Add tomatoes, chilies, salt and pepper. Add stock and milk and bring to a boil.
2. Reduce heat to simmer for 15 minutes.
   Add scallions, then seafood. Simmer 7 minutes covered. Add lime juice and cilantro; continue to simmer 5 more minutes.

Serves 16.

Undine's Winter Bean Stew

Butch Parilo – *Undine Barge Club Chef*

Over the years more and more Club members have asked for vegetarian dishes so I try to have a vegetarian main course each month. For the October Pasta Diner there is a vegetarian pasta dish and half of the antipasti are meatless. Even in March, the Bouillabaisse is accompanied by a Spinach Salad, which makes a delicious vegetarian meal.

My mother's bean soup was wonderful but my bean soup is legendary. But both are made with ham, a ham bone and chicken stock. As my mother did, I make my bean soup amass, using the leftover Easter ham and bone then freeze it in smaller batches for use over the winter.

This dish is made without ham and with water instead of chicken stock. The addition of Kale does change the nature of the soup – stew. It also means that it does not freeze (or defrost) well and is just not the same after a day or two. It's still good and well worth eating but the freshness of the Kale is lost if not eaten soon after its addition. So, I make it in two stages. The Kale is an important element in making this a great stew, so do a little exploratory shopping beforehand if you are serious about making this dish. I have found that Wholefoods' Kale selection is unmatched for freshness and variety. They are expensive but this dish is generally inexpensive so I don't mind splurging to make it the best I can.

This dish is a great accompaniment to the December Dinner's main course, which pays homage to the Club's German heritage, Crown Roast with pork stuffing and gravy. No one goes away hungry!

INGREDIENTS
Table salt
1 pound of dried cannellini beans
½ ounce dried porcini mushrooms
½ gallon spring or filtered water
Extra virgin olive oil
1 large onion, chopped medium pieces
2 large carrots, peeled and cut into ½ inch pieces
2 large celery ribs, cut into ½ inch pieces

5 garlic cloves, crushed or minced (more if you like)
1 large bay leaf
1 28-ounce can diced tomatoes, drained
1 pound good quality kale, stems removed and chopped into bite size pieces
1 sprig rosemary
Parmesan cheese

DIRECTIONS

1. Two days before the meal soak beans overnight in a gallon of water with 4 tablespoons of salt.
2. One day before the meal, drain and rinse the beans. Put dried porcinis into a bowl and pour about ½ cup of boiling water over them. Let sit for about 5 minutes or until soft, lift mushrooms from bowl and chop. Reserve mushroom water for later.
3. Over medium heat cover the bottom of a heavy pot with olive oil and heat for a minute or two, add onions, carrots and celery. Cook until vegetables are soft and have some color, about 10 minutes. Add garlic and cook about one to two minutes. Add water, bay leaf, soaked beans, mushrooms and mushroom water being careful not to pour in the grit at the bottom of the bowl. Cover pot and cook until beans are tender and start to crack about 1½ hour or more.
4. Taste the beans, taste several beans if you are making this to be served immediately. The beans should be done to your likening, if they are not, keep cooking and tasting until they are. Taste for salt and pepper. Since I am making this for the next day and will have to bring the soup (it's not stew yet) back up to a boil I don't want the beans to be real mushy but I do like them soft. When that happens, I'll stop, remove the pot from the heat and cool in a sink of cold water, refrigerate and finish the next day.
5. The day of the dinner, allow soup to come to room temperature before putting on heat. Bring soup to a simmer stirring often; simmer for about 10 minutes to be sure it is hot and ready to have the kale added. Add tomatoes, kale and rosemary; cook about 30 more minutes. Taste the kale, when it is tender the stew (yes, now it is stew) is finished. Serve with extra virgin oil drizzled on top, Parmesan cheese and Undine's garlic bread.

Serves 8–10.

Bouillabaisse

....

Butch Parilo – *Undine Barge Club Chef*

....

Late March can be a strange time, the lion or lamb thing. We could still have some winter or start feeling spring. So, I needed a dish for the March dinner that was hearty yet somewhat light. Bouillabaisse!

Ray Del Bianco wanted an Irish dinner in March for St. Patty's Day. I told him to call this Irish Fish Stew, hey its Joe McFadden's favorite dinner; you cannot get more Irish than that.

This is a combination of several recipes and years of trial and error. If you're a cook you've read and heard many times buy 'fresh'. Buy fresh, whole, clear-eyed, red gilled fish and have your monger filet and remove the skin, gills and fins. Have him cut up the frame into two or three pieces depending on your pot size. The Club has been enjoying Bouillabaisse each March for about twenty years and I always make too much!

INGREDIENTS
2 pounds fresh flounder, cut into small pieces. Do not marinade the flounder
  or count it in your 20 pounds.
20 pounds more fish including shrimp, scallops (large, dry, cut in half), red snapper,
  sea bass, ling, monk, haddock, halibut. If possible, get at least two fish frames. No
  squid — it gets too tough. You should have at least 12 pounds of fish with up to 8
  pounds of shrimp and scallops.

INGREDIENTS – Marinade
4 tablespoons of sea salt, fleur de sel, or gray salt — yes, it matters; everything matters
1 tablespoon of crushed red pepper flakes
10 to 12 cloves of garlic, minced fine or pressed
1 cup fresh basil, chiffonade
½ cup Pernod
1 heaping tablespoon of saffron threads
Extra virgin olive oil, to cover and mix with above and fish/shellfish

INGREDIENTS – Stock

3 fennel bulbs, remove stalks, bottom, any brown spots and chop into medium pieces
4 large carrots, chopped into medium pieces
4 to 6 Vidalia or other sweet onions, depending on size, peeled and quartered
2 large bulbs of garlic, outer paper removed and cut in half horizontally
4 large leeks, remove only very dark parts, split length ways rinsed and chopped
1 bunch of parsley, stems included
1 small bunch of thyme, about half the bunch you buy in a supermarket
6 bay leaves
12 whole black peppercorns
2 tablespoons sea salt
4 35-ounce cans of Tuttorosso's diced tomatoes
Extra Virgin Olive oil
Shrimp shells
2 to 3 bottles of a really good white wine. I go to Phillips Fine Wine on Bridge St.,
  Stockton, NJ when I need a good wine for this dish. Also, put this wine on the table.
Whole peel from one large orange no white

DIRECTIONS – Marinade

1. Clean and peel the shrimp, save the shells for stock.
2. Get rid of the little tough piece on the scallop and cut in half.
3. Cut up the fish filets into pieces that are about twice the size that will fit comfortably on a soupspoon, not to small, they will break up.
4. In a large bowl, mix shrimp, scallops and fish with salt, pepper, garlic, basil, Pernod, saffron and olive oil. Cover and put in refrigerate for about 6 hours.

DIRECTIONS – Stock

1. Rinse the fish frames and heads.
2. Using a pot large enough to hold everything, cover the bottom of the pot with olive oil, add fennel, carrots, and onions, let warm. When you think they are warm place the fish frames and heads on top, cover and check after ten minutes.
3. Sweat the frames and heads. You want to actually see beads of sweat on the fish heads. Keep the heat on the low side and do not burn the vegetables.
4. When the fish has started to sweat, add garlic, leeks, parsley, thyme, peppercorns, sea salt, tomatoes, shrimp shells and wine.
5. Add water to cover well. This is your soup. Later you will add all the fish to the finished stock. Also, too much water is okay, as you will reduce it later to concentrate the flavor.

6. Bring the stock to a simmer, uncovered over medium to high heat but do not boil. Turn heat down a little and keep it at a low simmer for an hour from the time it started simmering, add water if needed. Do not overcook, it will get bitter. Do not boil, as it will get cloudy.
7. After simmering for one hour strain the stock pressing lightly on the bones and stuff. You will want to strain out as much of the solids as possible. I strain it twice; first in a colander and then through a cheesecloth. Pick the meat from the bones and heads. If you are reusing the original pot, wipe it out before returning the strained stock.

DIRECTIONS – Finishing the Soup
1. Put the stock in a clean pot. Now is the time to consider if you should add more water, remembering all the fish must fit comfortably within the stock to make a soup.
2. Add the flounder and bring to a gentle boil, reduce the stock a little to concentrate the flavor. Use a wooden spoon to break up the flounder. Do not add the Marinating fish yet. When reduction is completed move the pot off the heat.
3. Add the orange peel, cover and let infuse until you are ready to cook the fish and serve. The above can be made several hours ahead. Your timing will depend on how quickly you can get the stock up to a rolling boil. The fish will only take about ten minutes to cook.
4. Take out the orange peel, put the stock on high heat and bring to a rolling boil because when you add the cold fish it will cool the whole process down a little.
5. Add all the fish, keep the heat on high, stir a few times and watch the shrimp. When the shrimp start to turn pink you have about five minutes to go. At this point turn off the heat and cover. The soup will be ready in two to five minutes.

This is all about timing and getting the fish just done and on the table because the fish keeps on cooking in the hot soup. So, check the other fish, do not overcook or undercook the fish. And taste it, let everyone it the kitchen taste it, add a little salt if needed. Add some more Pernod if you like. There are several orange liquors you could add if you like. Serve in warm tureens.

Serves 40+.

Main Dishes

Crustless Quiche

Mrs. Albert L. Doering III – *married an oarsman 49 years ago, raised three children who all rowed and likes to cook!*
University Barge Club

INGREDIENTS
4 eggs, unbeaten
½ cup onions, chopped, sautéed in 2 tablespoons butter
6–7 pieces or bacon, cooked, crumbled or left over ham
4 ounces Swiss or Cheddar cheese, grated/shredded
¼ cup of flour
1½ cup of milk, cream or non-fat milk

DIRECTIONS
1. Preheat oven to 350° F. Butter a 10 inch pie plate. Sprinkle grated cheese on plate.
2. In a bowl, blend eggs, flour and milk for 1 minute with electric mixer. Pour egg mixture in pie plate. Sprinkle with bacon and onions on top.
3. Bake for about 35 minutes. Let stand for 5 minutes before serving.

Serves 6.

Many variations of this make it a great recipe when stuck for dinner. Shrimp can be used instead of the bacon. Add spinach or broccoli for health and color.
This is a great meal to serve when the refrigerator seems empty. There are always a few things you can put into the basic egg & cheese mixture to make it tasty.

Chicken Corn Chowder

Mrs. Albert L. Doering, III
University Barge Club

INGREDIENTS
1½ cup half and half
1 cup chicken broth
1 10¾-ounce can condensed cream of potato soup
1 10¾-ounce can cream of celery soup
2 cups chicken, cooked, shredded (4 large breast halves)
⅓ cup green onions, chopped
1 11-ounce can corn with red peppers, including liquid
1 4-ounce can sliced mushrooms, including liquid
1 4-ounce can chopped green chilies
1½ cup sharp Cheddar cheese, shredded

DIRECTIONS
In a large saucepan, combine all ingredients. Stir together well and heat until hot. Do not boil! Can be doubled.

Serves 6.

Has been called "Dump" Soup since the hardest part is opening the cans to dump the ingredients into the pan.

Spicy Noodles

Gail and Jeff Lahm
Passaic River Rowing Association

INGREDIENTS
½ cup soy sauce
2 tablespoon white vinegar
4 tablespoons peanut butter
1 teaspoon ginger, fresh, grated
4 tablespoons sesame oil
1 teaspoon red pepper, crushed, more to taste
4 cloves garlic, chopped
1 pound linguini, cooked, whole wheat is best
Garnish optional: chopped peanuts, cilantro or scallions

DIRECTIONS
In a large serving bowl, combine all ingredients. Garnish with chopped peanuts, parsley, cilantro or scallions.

Serves 4.

Chicken Fesenjoon
(Chicken in Walnut and Pomegranate Sauce)

Robert Fallahnejad
Vesper Boat Club | Harrington High School | Penn AC | Columbia University

INGREDIENTS
2 tablespoons olive oil, ghee or butter
2 medium onions, finely chopped
1 pound bone-in chicken thighs, legs, and/or breasts, skin removed
½ pound walnuts, shells removed, finely ground
4 cups pomegranate juice or ½ cup pomegranate syrup/molasses
  diluted in 2 cups of water
¼ teaspoon saffron (optional)
Salt, to taste
Honey or sugar
Juice and pulp of 1 lemon
Pinch of allspice (optional)

DIRECTIONS
1. Heat the oil in a large pan or Dutch oven over medium heat. Add the onion and cook until tender, about 10–15 minutes. Remove onions.
2. Salt chicken. Add chicken to onions and brown on both sides, about three minutes per side. Remove from pan, and set aside.
3. Place the ground walnuts in the remaining oil in the pan. Cook and stir over low heat 5 to 10 minutes or until lightly browned. To grind walnuts, use a food processor, coffee grinder or a plastic bag and pulverize.
4. Return the onion and chicken to the frying pan with the walnuts. Stir in the pomegranate juice or diluted pomegranate syrup. Reduce heat to low, cover, and simmer 20 to 30 minutes, stirring occasionally, until chicken is no longer pink and juices run clear. You can simmer longer to deepen the flavor, adding water as necessary so the pan doesn't dry out.
5. Adjust seasoning to taste. If stew tastes too sour, add a little honey or sugar and simmer a bit longer. Serve over rice.

Makes 4 to 6 servings or feeds 2 heavyweights.

Spicy Slow-Cooker Vegetarian Chili

Dennis Egen
Malta Boat Club

INGREDIENTS
1 19-ounce can black bean soup, I use Progresso
1 15-ounce can kidney beans, rinsed and drained
1 15-ounce can garbanzo beans, rinsed and drained
1 16-ounce can vegetarian baked beans — Bush's is best
1 14.5-ounce can chopped tomatoes in purée
1 15-ounce can whole kernel corn, drained
1 onion, chopped
1 green bell pepper, chopped
2 Jalapeños, chopped
Add a combination of any of the following peppers:
2 Habañeros and/or 2 Serranos & 2 Pablanos or Cubanelles
  or Cubanos or Long Hots
2 stalks celery, chopped
2 tablespoons Garlic, minced
4 tablespoon chili powder, or to taste
2 tablespoon dried parsley
2 tablespoon dried oregano
2 tablespoon dried basil
Shredded Cheddar (optional)

DIRECTIONS
1. In a slow cooker, combine black bean soup,
   kidney beans, garbanzo beans, baked beans, tomatoes, corn, onion, peppers and celery.
   Season the soup with garlic, chili powder, parsley, oregano and basil.
2. Cook for at least six hours in slow cooker on low. Serve with melted Cheddar cheese, if desired.

Serves 8.

Aunt Anne Spinelli's Marinara Sauce

Mike DiLucca
Bachelors Barge Club | Conestoga Crew Club

INGREDIENTS
1 cup olive oil
4 garlic cloves, minced
5 carrots, peeled
4 celery stalks, strip off strings with vegetable peeler
Black pepper
Salt
Two, 6-pound 10-ounce cans of Italian peeled tomatoes with basil
Butter or chicken drippings for taste (optional)

DIRECTIONS
1. Place olive oil and garlic in a large spaghetti pot and heat, about 3 minutes.
2. While garlic is cooking, in a food processor combine carrots and celery. Process until finely chopped.
3. Add vegetable mixture to the garlic and oil. Add salt, a bit or so. Add about 5 shakes of black pepper. Cook for a short time on high until mixture slightly bubbles.
4. In a food processor, purée the 2 cans of tomatoes. Add to garlic and vegetable mixture. Using tomato can, add approximately 1 cup water to pot. Bring to a boil. Turn heat down to a simmer. Cook until desired consistency. When re-heating, add a little butter and salt to taste.

Serves lots of hungry rowers.

You can cut the recipe in half. The more carrots you add the sweeter the sauce.

Cottage Pie

April Roach
Vesper Boat Club

INGREDIENTS

2½ pounds ground beef (or use lamb to make Sheperd's Pie)
1 medium onion, chopped
2 medium–large tomatoes, peeled and chopped
4 medium carrots, peeled and chopped
⅓ cup small green olives, stuffed with pimientos, sliced
2½ pounds potatoes, cooked and mashed
Butter for making the mashed potatoes
Salt and freshly ground pepper
Herbs (fresh if possible):
 parsley, tarragon, rosemary, sage, basil, thyme, oregano, marjoram
Olive oil for sautéing vegetables

DIRECTIONS

1. Prepare mashed potatoes: peel, boil and mash with milk and butter. Season with salt, set aside.
2. Boil carrots until al dente, set aside.
3. Sauté onions in olive oil for a few minutes until soft. Add ground beef and tomatoes. Season the mixture with salt, pepper and herbs. Brown meat. Taste and adjust seasoning. Do not overcook. Remove from stove. Drain if necessary.
4. Mix in carrots and olives.
5. Spoon mixture into 3-quart casserole dish. Cover with mashed potatoes.
6. Bake in a 375°F oven for 15 minutes or until hot all the way through. May decorate with a sprig of parsley.

Serves 6–8.

Pasta Abruzzo

Lisa Adams
Great Bridge Crew

INGREDIENTS
Butter for greasing baking dish
2 cups red cherry or grape tomatoes, halved
2 cups yellow cherry or grape tomatoes, halved
¼ cup capers, rinsed and drained
1 tablespoon extra-virgin oil, plus extra for drizzling
½ teaspoon kosher salt, plus extra for seasoning
¼ teaspoon freshly ground pepper, plus extra for seasoning
½ cup Italian flavor breadcrumbs
1 pound ziti or short tube pasta
1¼ cups Pecorino Romano Cheese, grated
¼ cup fresh flat-leaf parsley, chopped

DIRECTIONS
1. Place oven rack in center of oven. Preheat oven to 375° F. Butter 8 × 8 inch glass baking dish.
2. In prepared baking dish, place tomatoes, capers, olive oil, salt and pepper. Toss to coat. Sprinkle the breadcrumbs over the tomato mixture. Drizzle the top with olive oil and bake for 30–35 minutes, until the top is golden. Cool for 5 minutes.
3. While tomato mixture is baking, bring large pot of salted water to a boil over high heat. Add the pasta and cook until tender but still firm to the bite, stirring occasionally, about 8–10 minutes. Drain and reserve about 1 cup of the pasta water.
4. Place pasta in a large serving bowl. Spoon the tomato mixture over the pasta. Add cheese and toss well. Thin out sauce with a little pasta water, if needed. Season sauce with salt and pepper to taste. Sprinkle with chopped parsley and serve immediately.

Serves 4–6.

Turkey Meatloaf

Kris Benarcik
Wilmington Rowing Center

INGREDIENTS

2 teaspoons vegetable oil
1 cup onion, finely chopped
¾ cup carrots, finely chopped
½ cup green onions, finely chopped
½ cup celery, finely chopped
½ cup red bell pepper, finely chopped
2 garlic cloves, minced
2½ pounds turkey breast, ground, uncooked
1 cup dry breadcrumbs
½ cup ketchup
1 teaspoon salt
1 teaspoon pepper
¼ teaspoon ground nutmeg
¼ teaspoon ground cumin
¼ teaspoon ground coriander
4 egg whites, lightly beaten
Vegetable cooking spray
½ cup ketchup
3 tablespoons brown sugar

DIRECTIONS

1. Preheat oven to 350° F. Coat 9 × 5 inch loaf pan with cooking spray.
2. Heat oil in large nonstick skillet over medium heat. Add onion, carrots, green onions, celery, red bell pepper and garlic. Sauté for 5 minutes, or until vegetables are tender. Remove from heat.
3. In a large bowl, combine onion mixture, turkey, breadcrumbs, ½ cup ketchup, salt, pepper, nutmeg, cumin, coriander and eggs; stir well.
3. Shape meat mixture into prepared pan. Place on a broiler pan coated with cooking spray. Bake for 30 minutes.
4. In a small bowl, combine ½ cup ketchup and brown sugar; brush over turkey loaf. Bake an additional 30 minutes or until internal temperature is 165° F. Let stand 10 minutes before slicing.

Serves 12.

Surprise Pasta Sauce

Kris Benarcik
Wilmington Rowing Center

INGREDIENTS
3 tablespoons olive oil
1 yellow onion, chopped
3 cloves garlic, minced
1 28-ounce can crushed tomatoes
1 28-ounce can plum tomatoes
2 tablespoons tomato paste
8 to 10 prunes, chopped
1 bay leaf
¼ to ½ teaspoon red pepper flakes, crushed
1½ tablespoons basil, chopped fresh or 1 teaspoon dried
2 tablespoon fresh parsley, chopped
1 teaspoon salt
Freshly ground pepper
Pasta of choice

DIRECTIONS
1. Heat olive oil in a heavy saucepan or Dutch oven over medium heat. Add onion; cook, stirring often, until softened, about 4 minutes. Add garlic; cook, stirring, 1 minute. Add tomatoes, paste, prunes, bay leaf and red pepper. Heat to a boil; reduce heat to simmer. Cook, stirring often, 1 hour.
2. Add basil and parsley; simmer 2 minutes. Remove bay leaf. Season sauce with salt and freshly ground pepper to taste.
3. Serve over pasta of choice.

Serves 8.

Fresh Herb Risotto

Maggie Brokaw
Wilmington Rowing Center

INGREDIENTS
7 cups vegetable stock
4 garlic cloves, minced
2 cups fresh herbs, chopped, such as parsley, chives, chervil, dill, basil, chives and arugula (approximately 4 cups leaves)
2 tablespoons olive oil
⅔ cup onion, chopped
Salt to taste
1½ cups Arborio rice
½ cup dry white wine
½ cup Parmesan cheese, freshly grated
Fresh ground pepper
Juice of ½ lemon (optional)

DIRECTIONS
1. In a stockpot, bring vegetable stock to a simmer on the stove.
2. In a bowl, combine the herbs and one of the minced garlic cloves; set aside.
3. In a wide and heavy skillet, heat olive oil over medium heat. Add the onion and ½ teaspoon salt. Cook until just tender and translucent, about 3 minutes. Stir in the rice and 3 cloves of garlic. Stir just until grains of rice separate and crackle. Add wine and cook, stirring, until it is absorbed. Adjust heat as needed to keep at a simmer.
4. Begin adding the simmering stock ½ cup at a time. Stir often, adding another ½ cup each time the rice has absorbed most of the liquid. When the rice is tender but still chewy, usually in 20 to 25 minutes, it is done. Add salt to taste.
5. Add another ¼ cup of stock and stir in the herbs, pepper, Parmesan and lemon juice (optional);
   add more stock if needed. Remove from the heat. Cover for a few minutes. It should be creamy and is best served immediately.

Serves 4.

Spaghetti Carbonara

Janet Bellantoni
Berkeley Paddling and Rowing Club | Vesper Boat Club

INGREDIENTS
1 pound dried spaghetti
4 eggs + 1 yolk, at room temperature
¾ cup Parmesan cheese, grated
12 ounces bacon
½ teaspoon black pepper
Salt to taste

DIRECTIONS
1. Cook bacon in frying pan until done, but not quite crisp, approximately 10 minutes. Remove bacon from pan but save bacon grease. Chop bacon coarsely and set aside.
2. In a bowl, briefly mix eggs, cheese and black pepper.
3. In a large pot, cook pasta until al dente and drain.
4. Put pasta back into the cooking pot and coat with some of the remaining bacon grease. Pour in the egg mixture and stir. The heat of the pasta should sufficiently cook the egg, but a low flame can be used for a minute or two to gain the appropriate consistency. The eggs should be warmed through, but still shiny. Stir in bacon; add salt and pepper to taste. This dish should be served immediately and enjoyed hot.

Serves 4.

Pot Roast

Bill Skowronski
Bachelors Barge Club

INGREDIENTS

3 pounds pot roast
2 tablespoons canola oil
1 small can tomato paste
2 cans Campbell's Beef Consommé
1 garlic clove, minced
Garlic powder
Seasoned pepper
Paprika
Salt
½ cup cream or dry sherry
1 teaspoon brown sugar
6 carrots, cut at diagonal
6 potatoes, cut in chunks
4 onions, cut in chunks

DIRECTIONS

1. In a small bowl, mix consommé and tomato paste thoroughly. Add brown sugar and sherry. Set aside.
2. In a frying pan, brown meat in oil with garlic then place meat and garlic in a roasting pan. Season meat with pepper, garlic powder, paprika and salt.
3. In the meat juices, heat consommé mixture. Pour heated consommé mixture over meat. Add vegetables.
4. Roast covered at 325° F for 3 hours.
5. When done, remove meat and allow to stand for 5 minutes. Cut at a diagonal. Pour gravy over meat.

Serves 4.

Sesame Noodles

Bachelors Barge Club

INGREDIENTS
12 ounces whole wheat spaghetti
1 tablespoon toasted sesame oil
2 cloves garlic, minced
1 tablespoon ginger, grated
2 tablespoons balsamic vinegar
4 tablespoons lower-sodium soy sauce
2 tablespoons brown sugar
14 ounces extra firm tofu, drained
  OR 3 boneless, skinless chicken breasts
1 tablespoon canola oil
4 scallions, sliced
1 hot red chili pepper, thinly sliced (optional)
⅓ cup unsalted crunchy peanut butter
4 cups romaine lettuce, shredded

DIRECTIONS
1. Cook spaghetti in a large pot of boiling water until tender but still firm. Drain and return to pot, reserving ⅓ cup of the hot pasta water. Toss the spaghetti with the sesame oil and set aside.
2. While pasta is cooking, mix garlic, ginger, vinegar, soy sauce and sugar in a medium bowl. Slice the tofu into 5 slabs, then cut slabs diagonally to make 10 triangles (or cut the chicken into 1 inch cubes). Blot the tofu with a paper towel.
3. Heat canola oil in a large non-stick skillet over medium heat. Sauté tofu (or chicken) until golden brown, about 2 minutes. Turn tofu over then add 3 tablespoons of the soy sauce mixture to the pan. Sauté until the sauce is absorbed by the tofu. Remove from heat and toss in the scallions and chilies.
4. Whisk the peanut butter and ⅓ cup of the hot pasta water into the remaining soy sauce mixture. Pour peanut butter and soy sauce mixture over spaghetti and toss. Serve immediately on a bed of shredded romaine lettuce, topped with the tofu (or chicken).

Serves 4–5.

Turkey Chili

Cheryl Cook
University Barge Club

INGREDIENTS

4 tablespoons olive oil, divided
1 medium onion, rough chopped
2 medium red bell peppers, rough chopped
3 cloves garlic, divided
1 pound plum tomatoes, chopped and seeded
  OR 1 28-ounce can plum tomatoes
1 15-ounce can corn, drained and rinsed
Kosher salt and fresh ground pepper
½ cup shredded cheese of choice
1 15-ounce can black beans, drained and rinsed
1 pound ground turkey
2 teaspoon cinnamon
½ cup cilantro, chopped
Grated cheese for topping

DIRECTIONS

1. In a Dutch oven, heat half of oil, sauté onion until translucent. Add half of garlic, sauté another minute. Add peppers. Cook until soft and brown at edges. Add tomatoes and simmer.
2. In separate sauté pan, heat remaining olive oil over medium heat, sauté remaining garlic. Add ground turkey and sauté until brown. Liberally salt and pepper.
3. Add ground turkey mixture to tomato mixture. Add canned corn and beans. Simmer until heated through. Add cinnamon and stir. Add cilantro and stir. Serve topped with grated cheese.

Serves 4.

Chicken Marengo

Onie Rollins
Wilmington Rowing Center

INGREDIENTS

6–8 boneless chicken breasts, cut into bite-size pieces
½ cup flour
Tarragon to taste
Olive oil
1 cup dry white wine
2 cups canned tomatoes, diced with liquid
1 cup mushrooms, sliced

DIRECTIONS

1. Preheat oven to 350° F.
2. In a medium bowl, mix tarragon with flour and coat chicken pieces. Reserve any extra flour.
3. In a frying pan, brown chicken quickly in olive oil. Place chicken in an ovenproof casserole dish using a slotted spoon. Top with mushrooms.
4. In frying pan with cooked juices, add reserved flour. Over medium heat, gradually whisk in wine and canned tomatoes. When thick, pour over chicken and mushrooms.
5. Bake in covered casserole dish for about 50 minutes. Serve over brown rice.

Serves 6.

Bolognese

Butch Parilo – *Undine Barge Club Chef*

INGREDIENTS

1 pound diced pancetta; do not use bacon

2 pounds carrots, minced

2 pounds Vidalia onions, minced (if available, if not use any sweet onion)

1 whole stalk of celery, minced (a big stalk, do not use dark leaves). I say minced instead of diced because the minced vegetables will disintegrate and become unrecognizable in the sauce easier than if diced.

5 pounds ground pork

5 pounds ground beef—not lean

4 pounds ground Veal. Find a good butcher, do not go through all this trouble and use supermarket meats. I use Rieker's Prime Meats: 7979 Oxford Avenue, Phila.

1 bottle of a good dry wine, white or red; whichever you prefer. I use one of the Gallo's Reserve whites. A good wine will help but a really great wine will be lost in this dish.

10 large cloves garlic, minced

2 large cans of tomato paste diluted with an equal amount of beef broth/stock. I use American's test kitchen as a source for the best products. They are currently recommending Rachael Ray's Stock-in-a-box made by Colavita or College Inn beef stock.

2 35-ounce cans of Tuttorosso crushed tomatoes, add more for a sweeter sauce

Salt and Pepper, taste and add as you cook the sauce

3 cups whole milk

2 cups heavy cream

½ pound Parmesan Reggiano, grated

½ pound of Locatelli Pecorino Romano, grated. I mix these two together.

6–7 pounds of rustic rigatoni or pappardelle pasta

DIRECTIONS

1. Preheated your oven to 375° F.
2. In a non-stick saucepan slowly reduce the two cups of heavy cream to one cup.
3. In a large heavy pot capable of holding all the ingredients and being placed in the oven, slowly render the pancetta over medium heat until crisp. Adjust heat so fat does not smoke and burn during rendering. When pancetta is crisp add the carrots, onions and celery. Sauté until all the vegetables are soft.

....

4. While vegetables are cooking, combine meats in a large mixing bowl and season lightly with salt and pepper. When vegetables are soft, raise heat to medium high, and start adding the meat mixture in small pieces, so as not to create clumps. Cook meat until medium brown, not dark. After all the meat is added and browned, add the tomato paste and beef broth/stock mixture, stir to incorporate. Add the garlic, wine and crushed tomatoes; stir to incorporate.

5. Bring to a boil, lower heat to simmer and cook for fifteen minutes.

6. Put the pot in the preheated oven uncovered.

7. About every fifteen minutes slide out the rack with the pot and; first skim all the surface fat, second add about a half cup of milk and stir, slide rack and pot back into oven. Repeat until all milk is incorporated, about two hours. The last addition of milk should be allowed to cook into sauce. The chef told me that this will draw out the moisture, along with skimming off the fat, replacing the lost moisture with milk and finishing with reduced cream, creates a rich sauce.

8. To finish remove sauce from oven, skim again, add reduced cream, and stir to incorporate the cream.

9. I serve this by first putting the cooked pasta (a pound at a time) in a large mixing bowl, ladling some of the Bolognese, stirring, adding more if needed to cover all the pasta without having the pasta swimming in sauce. The large hole in the rigatoni will suck up some of the sauce. Add more Bolognese until you are satisfied with the coverage, the n throw in a small handful of the grated cheese mixture and mix again. Put the sauced pasta into a large serving dish and top with some more cheese, drizzle with some very good extra virgin olive oil and serve.

Serves 25.

Million Dollar Chicken

Malta Boat Club

INGREDIENTS

3 cups hot cooked rice
1 tablespoon olive oil
¼ cup almonds, coarsely chopped
2 garlic cloves, minced
2 chicken breasts, chopped
¼ cup water
1 cup salsa
2 tablespoons dried currants or raisins
1 tablespoon honey
¾ teaspoon ground cumin
½ teaspoon ground cinnamon

DIRECTIONS

1. Cook rice as directed on package.
2. Heat oil to medium high in a heavy frying pan. Add almonds, cook 1–2 minutes and remove, alternatively, toast them in the oven. Reheat frying pan, cook garlic for about 30 seconds then add the chicken. Turn once during cooking, after about 4–5 minutes then add salsa, water, currants/raisins, honey, cumin & cinnamon to cooking chicken. Reduce heat to medium, cook for 20 minutes.
3. Stir in almonds and serve with rice.

Serves 4.

Spring Vegetable Pesto Pasta

Bachelors Barge Club

INGREDIENTS
8 cloves garlic
⅓ cup pine nuts
¾ cup whole wheat fusilli or penne pasta
1 pound thin asparagus spears, trimmed and cut into 2 inch pieces
2 cups peas, fresh or thawed, divided 1½ cups and ½ cup
6 ounce basil, stems discarded, about 5 cups loosely packed
8 sprigs mint, stems discarded, about 1 cup loosely packed
1 ounce Parmesan cheese, freshly grated, ½–¾ cup depending on grate, divided in half
¼ cup extra-virgin olive oil
Freshly ground black pepper
1 teaspoon kosher salt, divided in half

DIRECTIONS
1. Preheat oven to 350° F.
2. Lightly brush or spray the garlic with oil. Roast garlic with the pine nuts on a baking sheet until the nuts are golden brown and the garlic has softened, about 12 minutes.
3. Boil the pasta in a large pot of water as directed on package. With 2 minutes remaining before the pasta is done, add the asparagus. Add 1½ cups peas when the pasta is done. Remove from heat, drain pasta and vegetables, reserving ½ cup of pasta water, and return them to the pot.
4. While the pasta is cooking, make the pesto. In a food processor, pulse the roasted garlic and pine nuts with the basil, mint, remaining ½ cup peas, half the Parmesan cheese and the oil until uniformly chopped. Season with pepper and ½ teaspoon salt. Add ½ cup of the pasta water to pesto and stir.
5. Toss the pasta and vegetables with the pesto. Serve immediately sprinkled with remaining salt and Parmesan cheese.

Serves 4.

Lentil Spaghetti Sauce

Gail Kachnycz and Carolyn Stub
Malta Boat Club

INGREDIENTS
½ cup canola oil
1 medium onion, chopped
1½ cup dried lentils, washed and picked over
2½ teaspoon salt
4 cups water
1 clove garlic, crushed
½ teaspoon pepper
4 beef or chicken bouillon cubes
1 green pepper, chopped
1 1-pound 12-ounce can tomatoes
1 6-ounce can tomato paste
1 4-ounce can mushrooms
Black or green olives
1 package Spatini spaghetti sauce mix
¼ teaspoon oregano
2 teaspoons vinegar
¼ teaspoon basil
1 green pepper, chopped

DIRECTIONS
1. In a large saucepan, cook onion in oil. When softened add lentils, salt, water, garlic, pepper and bouillon. Cover and simmer for 30 minutes.
2. Add remaining ingredients except green pepper. Simmer uncovered over low heat one hour.
3. In last 10 minutes add chopped green pepper.

Serves an army.

Serve over spaghetti or in Lentil Lasagna Florentine.

Lentil Lasagna Florentine

Gail Kachnycz
Malta Boat Club

INGREDIENTS

1 batch of lentil spaghetti sauce – see previous recipe
1 green pepper, chopped
1½ pound part-skim mozzarella cheese, sliced
1 10-ounce package of lasagna noodles, boiled
2 packages creamed spinach, boiled
Filling:
4½ cups cottage cheese, small curd, skim
¾ cup Parmesan cheese, grated
3 tablespoon parsley flakes
3 eggs, beaten
2 teaspoon salt
¾ teaspoon pepper

DIRECTIONS

1. Preheat oven to 350° F.
2. Spray 9 × 13 inch pan with cooking spray and arrange layers as follows: ⅓ of noodles, ½ lentil sauce, ½ cheese filling and ½ mozzarella slices. Another ⅓ of noodles, ½ cheese filling, and all of creamed spinach. Last ⅓ of noodles, other ½ lentil sauce and other ½ mozzarella slices.
3. Bake, covered with foil for 45 minutes. Remove foil after 30 minutes of baking. Lasagna is done when lightly brown and bubbly. Allow to stand 10–15 minutes before cutting.

Serves an army.

Pesce in Cartoccio
(Fish Baked in Parchment Paper)

Bachelors Barge Club

INGREDIENTS
6 teaspoon extra virgin olive oil
6 3 to 4-ounce portions of fish filets such as sea-bass, halibut, swordfish or salmon, about ½ inch thick
Salt to taste
Fresh ground pepper to taste
6 large basil leaves
1 lemon cut into 12 slices
1 ounce dry white wine
½ teaspoon red chili flakes (optional)

DIRECTIONS
1. Cut six pieces of parchment paper about 12 × 16 inch and fold in half to form a triangle. Place one fish filet near the fold.
2. Season with 1 teaspoon olive oil, salt, pepper, a basil leaf, squirt of lemon juice and a splash of wine but not too much. Plait, or fold, the paper shut. Tuck the last fold under the fish filet to hold closed. A staple works, too. This can be done several hours ahead of time.
3. Preheat oven to 400° F. Place a sheet pan or shallow roasting pan in the oven to get hot.
4. Carefully place the fish and parchment on the baking sheet, they should barely touch, and bake for about 10 minutes. The parchment bag should puff as the fish cooks.
5. When done, remove from oven and place packages on hot plates to serve immediately. Let the eater open the package by ripping open the top — the aroma is wonderful. Eat the fish right out of the paper.

Serves 6.

You can also let the packages cool completely, unwrap them and refrigerate them up to one day in advance. Serve cold. They are delicious with a generous sprinkling of red chili flakes.

Chicken Salad

Malta Boat Club

INGREDIENTS
2 cups cooked chicken, chopped
1 tablespoon curry
1 teaspoon salt
¾ teaspoon pepper
1 cup sour cream
3 stalks celery, chopped
2½ tablespoons mango chutney
¼ cup almonds, slivered (optional)

DIRECTIONS
In a medium bowl, combine curry, salt, pepper, sour cream, chutney and almonds. Mix well. Add chicken and celery. Enjoy on bread or crackers.

Serves 4.

Quiche

Malta Boat Club

INGREDIENTS
3 eggs
1½ cups milk
1½ cups cheese, shredded
1 small onion, chopped
6 pieces bacon, cooked and crumbled; can substitute ⅓ cup ham
1 package frozen spinach or other vegetable
½ teaspoon salt
Piecrust

DIRECTIONS
1. Preheat oven to 350° F.
2. In a medium bowl, combine all ingredients and pour into piecrust. Bake for 45 minutes.

Serves 6.

Lisa's Italian Shrimp Pasta

Malta Boat Club

INGREDIENTS
1 pound penne, bow tie or other pasta
2 pounds shrimp, peeled, deveined
2 tablespoons canola oil
1 onion, chopped
2–3 cloves garlic, minced
2 celery stalks, chopped
Dijon mustard to taste
Worcestershire Sauce to taste
2 15-ounce cans diced tomatoes, not seasoned
1 bell pepper, chopped
¼–½ cup white wine (optional)
⅓ cup grated Parmesan cheese

DIRECTIONS
1. In a large frying pan, sauté onion, garlic, celery, mustard and Worcestershire sauce. Simmer 10 minutes. Add shrimp and diced tomatoes, pepper, and white wine. Cook until shrimp is pink and done.
2. Meanwhile cook the pasta as directed on the package. Drain and transfer pasta to a large serving bowl. Pour shrimp sauce over the pasta. Sprinkle with grated Parmesan cheese. Serve with a salad and enjoy!

Serves 6.

Pork Tenderloin

Malta Boat Club

INGREDIENTS

3 1-pound pork tenderloins
5 tablespoons honey
5 tablespoons rum
8 tablespoons Dijon mustard
8 tablespoons apricot preserves
1 can apricot halves, drained

DIRECTIONS

1. Preheat oven to 425° F.
2. Rinse and pat dry pork tenderloin. Place pork in oven-safe dish and cook for 10 minutes. Add apricot halves and return to oven.
3. While meat is cooking, in a small saucepan, mix together honey, rum, mustard, and preserves. Simmer on low heat until mixture thickens. Pour half of this glaze over the meat 10 minutes after apricot halves are added. Cook tenderloin for 30–40 minutes total or until internal temperature is 160° F. Remove from oven, tent with foil and allow to rest for 10 minutes. Place meat on a serving platter and top with remaining glaze.

Serves 6–8.

Aunt Bonnie's Corned Beef

Margaret Meigs
University Barge Club

INGREDIENTS
3½ pounds corned beef brisket
2 bay leaves
6 peppercorns
Whole cloves
6 tablespoons oil
3 tablespoons mustard
1 cup brown sugar
9 tablespoons vinegar

DIRECTIONS
1. Wash the beef and place in a large Dutch oven or pot. Cover with water; add bay leaves and pepper. Over high heat, bring to a boil. Continue boiling for 5 minutes.
2. Skim surface, cover and reduce to a simmer. Simmer for 4 hours or until tender.
3. Remove meat and place in a shallow baking pan. Dot with whole cloves.
4. Preheat oven to 350° F.
5. In a small saucepan, combine remaining ingredients and heat, stirring until blended. Pour over meat. Bake for 30 minutes basting frequently.

Serves 6.

Basic Curry

INGREDIENTS
4–6 tablespoons Olive oil
1 teaspoon cumin seeds
4 medium onions, finely chopped
5 cloves garlic, finely chopped
1 tablespoon ginger, finely chopped
3 medium tomatoes, diced
A small sprig of fresh cilantro
1 teaspoon turmeric
1 teaspoon coriander powder
1 teaspoon cumin powder
1 teaspoon dried mango powder (found in Indian stores as "Amchur")
1 teaspoon paprika
½ teaspoon hot chili powder
½ teaspoon "Garam Masala" (found in Indian stores)
Salt to taste
Black pepper to taste (optional)
2 pounds (skinless) boneless chicken cut in small bite sized cubes
   OR 1 pound shrimp peeled and deveined

DIRECTIONS – Curry for Chicken or Shrimp

1. In a large saucepan, heat the oil and add cumin seeds. When the seeds start frying (you will hear popping and see it changing texture) add the onion, garlic and ginger. When they become golden brown, add tomatoes and cilantro leaves and immediately turn the heat to simmer and cover the saucepan for about five minutes until the tomatoes cook. At the end of this time remove the cover, turn up the heat and stir constantly to let the tomatoes caramelize in the high heat so that the reduction appears dark brown. This takes about five minutes. At this time quickly add all the spices, again stirring constantly, so that the spices do not char in the heat.

2. Immediately add chicken (or shrimp) and stir until the reduced gravy mix coats all the chicken. Turn the heat down to a simmer and cover the dish allowing the salt and spices to cook together with the chicken. Stir this mix occasionally cooking until the chicken is no longer pink.

3. When the chicken is done turn up the heat and add one cup of water to the saucepan, stir and bring the contents to a boil. Once the liquid boils, lower the heat to a low simmer for about 10 minutes. Serve the chicken over hot white basmati rice. Serves 6.

DIRECTIONS – Curry for Vegetables

Use 1 pound of any of the three options: a) green peas and paneer (homemade cheese found in Indian stores) b) cauliflower and potatoes or c) cut green beans and potatoes. Use all the ingredients of Basic Curry without meat, but reduce by half the amount of onion, ginger, garlic and tomato. Chop the veggies to bite sized pieces. Complete step 1 on previous page, but add the vegetables first instead of tomatoes. Once the onion, garlic and ginger are slightly brown add the vegetables, stir and lower heat to a simmer and cover saucepan. When vegetables are mostly tender or cooked through add the tomatoes, cilantro and all dry spices. Stir and cover until tomatoes are tender. Increase heat to high and stir until mixed. Serve hot with pita or Indian bread.

DIRECTIONS – Curry for Beef or Lamb

Additional ingredients:
2 pounds of beef or lamb cut to small bite sized cubes
3 cloves
1 cardamom
1 small inch-sized stick of cinnamon
3–4 black peppercorns
(The last four ingredients are found pre-mixed in correct proportions in the Indian stores as "garam masala" which one can freshly grind or, as in this recipe, use whole.)

1. Heat the oil and add cumin seeds. When the seeds start frying, add the meat, the additional "whole garam masala" spices: cloves, cardamom, cinnamon and peppercorns, followed by the onion, garlic and ginger. Add salt to taste at this stem as it acts as a meat tenderizer.
2. Increase heat to high for a minute and then reduce to simmer and cover. Check after about 20 minutes to see if meat is done. If the meat is not fork-tender, continue cooking until it is.
3. When meat is done, increase temperature and brown meat and the onion, garlic, ginger mixture. Continue to stir over high heat until all the meat is coated, slightly brown and oil is separating from the meat.
4. Add all the rest of the ingredients of the "Basic Curry" and stir over high heat for five minute until the contents are well blended. Add one cup of water and bring to boil. Lower heat and simmer for ten minutes and serve over hot white basmati rice.

Braised Chicken with Olives, Raisins and Capers

Margaret Meigs
University Barge Club

INGREDIENTS

3 pounds chicken thighs, bone-in or boneless
2 teaspoons salt
¼ cup olive oil
½ teaspoon black pepper
¼ cup chopped garlic
½ teaspoon red pepper flakes
2 tablespoon dried oregano
1 cup dry white vermouth
1 cup golden raisins
½ cup brown sugar
½ cup capers
½ cup red wine vinegar
1 cup green olives, pitted, sliced
¼ cup cilantro, chopped

DIRECTIONS

1. In a mixing bowl, combine chicken salt, oil, pepper, garlic, red pepper flakes and oregano to marinate overnight or for at least a couple of hours.
2. Preheat oven to 400° F. In a 9 × 13 inch baking pan, arrange chicken in a single layer. Bake 30 minutes or until lightly browned.
3. In a medium pot, combine the vermouth, raisins, brown sugar, capers, vinegar, and olives and bring to a boil. Pour over the chicken and bake for an additional 30 minutes, basting several times with the liquid.
4. Sprinkle chicken with cilantro and serve.

Serves 6.

Marinated Grilled Pork Tenderloins
Adapted from Williams-Sonoma, Essentials of Grilling

Andrea Bonaccorsi
Pocock Rowing Center | Bachelors Barge Club

INGREDIENTS
2 pork tenderloins, about 2½ lb. total, trimmed
⅔ cup balsamic vinegar
⅓ cup olive oil
2 tablespoons soy sauce
4½ teaspoons golden brown sugar, firmly packed
¾ teaspoon freshly ground pepper
½ cup fresh rosemary, finely chopped
5 cloves garlic, chopped

DIRECTIONS
1. To make the balsamic-rosemary marinade, in a food processor, combine the vinegar, olive oil, soy sauce, brown sugar and pepper and pulse until blended. Add the rosemary and garlic and continue to process until fairly smooth.
2. Place the tenderloins in a non-reactive dish and pour the marinade over them. Cover and let stand at room temperature, turning occasionally, for up to 2 hours.
3. Grill the meat over the hottest part of a charcoal fire or directly over the heat elements of a gas grill. Turn every 4 to 5 minutes and baste with the marinade for up to 5 minutes before the meat is cooked to your liking, about 20 minutes total for medium. Insert an instant-read thermometer into the thickest part of the tenderloins; it should register 140°F. The temperature will rise another 5°–10°F while the meat is resting.
4. Transfer tenderloins to a carving board, cover loosely with aluminum foil and let rest for 5 minutes. Carve into slices across the grain and at an angle to the cutting board. Season with salt. Serve the tenderloins hot, warm or at room temperature.

Serves 5.

Tenderloins can also be cooked in the oven on a broiler pan. Just bake tenderloins at 350°F turning and basting every 5 minutes or so. Broil for a minute or two at the end to get a grilled effect.

Meatballs in Cranberry Pinot Noir Sauce

Barb Grudt – *1984 & 1988 Olympian*
University of Pennsylvania | Vesper Boat Club | Peddie School

INGREDIENTS

1 16-ounce can whole cranberry sauce
1 cup brown sugar
½ cup pinot noir
2 teaspoons hot Chinese mustard
2 pounds bite-size meatballs or enough to make one layer in a 13 × 9 inch pan

DIRECTIONS

1. Preheat oven to 375° F. Lightly oil a 9 × 13 inch baking dish.
2. Put one layer of meatballs in prepared baking dish.
3. In a medium saucepan, stir together cranberry sauce, brown sugar, pinot noir and hot Chinese mustard. Simmer over medium heat for 5 minutes.
4. Remove from heat and pour over meatballs. Bake meatballs and sauce for about 20 minutes or until meatballs are warmed through.

Serves 6.

British Columbia Salmon with Lemon and Dill

Patrick Walter – *3-time Canadian Olympian*
Victoria City Rowing Club

INGREDIENTS

1 pound salmon fillet (if bones present — remove)
1 lemon, thinly sliced
1 tablespoon olive oil or 4 tablespoons butter, melted
3 tablespoons lemon juice
½ teaspoon dried dill weed
Pinch garlic powder
Sea salt to taste
Freshly ground black pepper to taste

DIRECTIONS

1. Preheat oven to 400° F. Lightly grease a medium baking dish.
2. Arrange half the lemon slices in a single layer in the baking dish and top with salmon fillet. Mix the olive oil (or butter) and lemon juice in a small bowl, and drizzle over the salmon. Season with dill, garlic powder, sea salt, and pepper.
3. Bake 18–20 minutes or until salmon is easily flaked with a fork.

Serves 2 hungry rowers.

Turkey Chili

Linda Muri *started rowing at MIT and was a nine-time National Team member from 1991–2000.*

INGREDIENTS

This is a free-style recipe, very forgiving and flexible. Use what you have on hand to save a trip to the store.

2 pounds ground turkey
3 cloves garlic, minced or smashed
1 onion, chopped
1–3 chilies from a can of Chipotle chilies (smoked Jalapeños)
3 cans ground chunky style tomatoes
1 16-ounce jar salsa Verde
4 cans pinto beans (or bean of choice), drained
1 teaspoon oregano
½ teaspoon red chili flakes — for heat
1 teaspoon ground coriander
Salt to taste
Toppings (optional)
Grated Cheddar
Sour cream

DIRECTIONS

1. In a frying pan, brown ground turkey, drain, and set aside.
2. In a stockpot, sauté garlic and onion till cooked but not brown. Mash in one or more of the chipotles depending on how spicy you want the chili to be. The chipotles are fairly mellow, smokey with a little kick. Add in the cooked turkey. Stir in tomatoes, salsa, and beans. Season to taste with coriander, chili flakes, and salt.
3. Simmer for an hour, or longer to meld the flavors.

Serves lots.

Goes well with rice or cornbread.

Desserts

Grandma's Apple Pie

Mrs. Albert L. Doering, III *who married an oarsman!*
University Barge Club

INGREDIENTS
3 tablespoon butter
1 egg, beaten
½ cup sugar
½ cup flour
½ teaspoon baking powder
½ teaspoon salt
1 can apple, blueberry or cherry pie filling (readily available at most food stores)

DIRECTIONS
1. Preheat oven to 325° F.
2. Topping: In a mixer, cream butter, sugar and egg. Add flour, salt and baking powder.
2. Grease a casserole dish. Place canned fruit pie filling in prepared dish. Spread topping over filling and bake until top is light brown and filling is bubbly, about 35 minutes.

Serves 6.

If you keep a can of the filling on hand, this is a quick easy dessert that can be made on the spur of the moment. If for company, serve with vanilla or cinnamon ice cream.

Judi Dench Dessert of Pain Perdue au Chocolat

Karin Tetlow *began rowing after moving to the Art Museum area in 1998. High point was a receiving a Schuylkill Navy plaque in 2006 for rowing three headraces and a turn the stake race in the Hutchinson Cup (something very unlikely to be repeated.)*
Bachelors Barge Club | Vesper Boat Club

INGREDIENTS
1 8-ounce packet of semi-sweet chocolate chips or 8 oz of dark Belgian chocolate from Trader Joe's
½ cup sugar
6 tablespoons butter
15 ounces heavy cream
4–8 slices of white bread, less or more depending on how solid you want the dessert
3 eggs, beaten
2 tablespoons rum or whatever

DIRECTIONS
1. Place chocolate, cream, butter and sugar in a microwave-safe bowl. Heat in microwave for 5 minutes. Add ½ minute more until all ingredients are melted, but be careful they don't boil over. Alternatively, wait a couple of minutes, and then stir until the mixture is dark. Stir eggs and rum into chocolate mixture
2. Add bread slices, squishing down so no white of the bread shows. Add more bread if you want the dessert to be more solid.
3. Let sit at room temperature for 2 hours.
4. Refrigerate for 24 hours.
5. Cook at 350° F for 30+ minutes until you hear bubbling (it's only the eggs that need cooking).

Serves 6–8.

May be served with cream.

Chocolate Paté with Zinfandel and Berries

Mimi Hanks-Bell
Bachelors Barge Club

INGREDIENTS

1 pound bittersweet chocolate, good quality, chopped
¾ cup Zinfandel or other red wine
¼ cup whipping cream
2 pints berries — it's ok to use frozen raspberries or strawberries, but fresh is better
½ cup sugar, adjust for taste

DIRECTIONS

1. Combine chocolate, wine and cream in top of double boiler*. Melt over simmering water on low heat until mixture is just smooth, stirring constantly. Do not allow chocolate to get too warm. Remove from heat and whisk well.
2. Pour into an 8 × 4 inch loaf pan lined with wax paper. Refrigerate overnight. Before serving, unmold the pate and slice into 8 slices. It is easier to create clean slices if you dip the knife into hot water after each cut.
3. Purée berries and sugar in a blender or food processor until smooth.
4. To serve, make a pool of sauce on each of 8 serving plates. Slice pate and place a slice on top of each pool of sauce.

Serves 8 rowers, 12 regular portions.

* If you don't have a double boiler, you need to be able to nestle a metal bowl over a pan of steamy simmering water making sure water or steam does not touch chocolate. It's the steam that melts the chocolate.

This is an easy do-ahead recipe that only rowers should eat — very rich and very good. Serve this and you will be everyone's new best friend. Both the chocolate pate and berry sauce can be made ahead.

Pumpkin Cheesecake

Ulana Dubas
University Barge Club

INGREDIENTS

1½ cups graham cracker crumbs
4 tablespoons butter
¼ cup sugar
1½ pounds cream cheese, softened
1 14-ounce can sweetened condensed milk
1 14-ounce can pumpkin purée
4 eggs
2 teaspoons cinnamon
¼ teaspoon nutmeg
¼ teaspoon ground cloves
1½ cups whipping cream
¼ cup powdered sugar

DIRECTIONS

1. Preheat the oven to 350° F. Place the butter into a 10 or 12 inch springform pan and place in the oven until butter is melted. Stir in the graham cracker crumbs and sugar. Press the mixture into the bottom of the pan and halfway up the sides. Return to oven and bake for 10 minutes.
2. Filling: In a large mixer, combine the cream cheese and sweetened condensed milk. Beat at medium–high speed until well combined. Add the pumpkin purée, eggs, cinnamon, nutmeg, and ground cloves. Beat at medium speed until mixture is completely smooth, scraping the sides of the bowl (approximately 2–3 minutes). Pour the mixture into pan. Bake for 60 minutes.
3. Remove the cheesecake from the oven and place it on a wire rack to cool completely. Run a knife blade along the rim of the pan to release the edge of the cake. Do not remove the outer right of the springform pan yet. Then remove the outer ring of the springform pan and place the cheesecake in the refrigerator for 2–3 hours or overnight.
4. Topping: Before serving, prepare the whipped cream. Beat the whipping cream and powdered sugar together until stiff peaks form. Spread the whipped cream over the cheesecake, this will hide any cracks that formed while baking. Chill again until you're ready to serve. Enjoy!

Serves 12.

Rum Balls

Dale Parenti *is quite an accomplished dragon boat paddler and sculler*
Whitemarsh Boat Club

INGREDIENTS

1 12-ounce package vanilla wafers, pulverized
1½ cups pecans, walnuts, or hazelnuts, chopped
¾ cup powdered sugar
¼ cup cocoa
½ cup light rum
3 tablespoons light corn syrup
½ cup powdered sugar, for finishing

DIRECTIONS

1. In a food processor, pulverize vanilla wafers, chopped nuts, powdered sugar, and cocoa. Transfer to a large bowl. Stir in in rum and corn syrup to form a thick, sticky dough.
2. Grease hands lightly and shape dough into 1 inch balls. Roll in remaining powdered sugar.
3. Store rum balls in an airtight container for 2 to 3 days to develop flavor. Roll them again in confectioners' sugar before serving.

Makes 4 dozen.

WARNING: These are potent! Keep them away from the kids.

Mamma Millie's Lemon Ice Box Pie

Debbie Kiely *is a sculler from Florida who shares a favorite family recipe*
Lightwave

INGREDIENTS
1 9 inch graham cracker pie crust, chilled
1 15-ounce can Eagle Brand sweetened condensed milk
⅓ cup lemon juice
2 drops yellow food coloring
2–3 tablespoons lemon zest
3 egg, separated
¼ teaspoon cream of tarter
Whipped topping (optional)

DIRECTIONS
1. In a large bowl, combine condensed milk, lemon juice, food coloring and zest.
2. In a small bowl, beat egg whites and cream of tarter until peaks are stiff but not dry. Add beaten egg yolks into the egg whites. Gently fold into lemon mixture. Pour into prepared crust. Chill
   for about two hours. Add whipped topping, if desired.

Serves 8.

Sticky Toffee Pudding

Maggie Brokaw
Wilmington Rowing Center

INGREDIENTS

8 ounces prunes or dates, finally chopped
1 cup boiling water
½ cup unsalted butter, at room temperature
1 cup light brown sugar
4 large eggs
1 ¾ cups self-rising flour
2 tablespoons instant coffee crystals
1 teaspoon baking soda
Caramel Sauce:
2 cups heavy cream
1 cup packed secant sugar (or similarly flavorful & minimally refined brown sugar)
¼ cup unsalted butter
1 teaspoon vanilla (optional)
Salt to taste
Whipped cream

DIRECTIONS

1. Preheat oven to 350°F. Butter a 9 inch-diameter springform pan, though any similarly sized pan will work okay. For best results, line bottom of pan with buttered parchment.
2. Place chopped prunes in small bowl. Pour the boiling water over them and let soak for about an hour.
3. In a large mixer, blend butter and sugar. Add 2 eggs, one at a time, beating well after each. Add half of the flour and beat to blend. Repeat this with the remaining eggs and flour and beat until well blended.
4. Add the coffee and baking soda to the prune mixture and stir to dissolve the coffee. Add prune mixture to batter and beat to blend. Pour into prepared pan.
5. Place pan in a rimmed baking sheet. Bake until tester comes out clean, about 1 hour.

6. While cake is baking, prepare the caramel sauce. In a small–medium saucepan, bring cream, sugar, vanilla, and butter to a boil over medium–high heat, stirring frequently. Reduce heat to medium–low and simmer until reduced to 1¾ cups, stirring occasionally, about 15 minutes. Taste and add salt, if needed. Sauce can be made up to one day ahead. Cover with plastic wrap so plastic lies on the sauce to prevent skin from forming, and refrigerate. Rewarm over medium–low heat with frequent stirring.
7. Allow cake to cool until warm. Unmold and cut cake into wedges or square chunks. Serve warm with caramel sauce and whipped cream.

Serves 8–12.

E-Z Coconut Custard Pie

Bill Skowronski *assisted with Monsignor Bonner High School crew program.*
Bachelors Barge Club

INGREDIENTS
2 cups milk
⅔ cup sugar
½ cup Bisquick
4 eggs
¼ cup butter
1½ teaspoons vanilla extract
1 cup shredded coconut

DIRECTIONS
1. Preheat oven to 350° F. Grease a 9 inch pie plate.
2. In a mixing bowl blend milk, sugar, Bisquick, eggs, butter and vanilla on low speed for 3 minutes. Pour into prepared pie plate. Let stand for 5 minutes. Then sprinkle with coconut.
3. Bake for 40 minutes.

Serves 6–8.

No pie shell needed! The Bisquick will form its own crust.

Wacky Cake

Fran Greenglass
Wilmington Rowing Center

INGREDIENTS
1½ cups flour
1 cup sugar
3 tablespoons cocoa powder
1 teaspoons baking soda
½ teaspoon salt
1 tablespoon white vinegar
1 teaspoon vanilla
6 tablespoons corn oil
1 cup cold water

Peanut butter frosting (optional):
¼ cup butter, softened
½ cup creamy peanut butter
1 ½ tablespoons milk, or as needed
1 cup confectioners sugar

Without the frosting, this is a vegan (and totally delicious) cake!

DIRECTIONS
1. Preheat oven to 350° F.
2. Cake: in a mixing bowl, combine flour, sugar, cocoa powder, baking soda and salt together. Add the vinegar, vanilla, oil and water and mix well (electric mixer works best).
3. Pour into ungreased 9 x 9 inch pan. Bake for 30 minutes.
4. Frosting: in an electric mixing bowl, cream butter and peanut butter together. Gradually mix in the sugar, and when it starts to get thick, incorporate milk, a little bit at a time, until all of the sugar is mixed in and the frosting is thick and spreadable. Continue to beat until frosting is fluffy, at least 3 minutes.

Serves about 9.

Never Fail Coffee Cake

Judy Kaplow *is a former music teacher in the Philadelphia Public Schools, Membership Director and Board Member for Masters Rowing Association and competitive rower.*
Vesper Boat Club

INGREDIENTS
2¼ cup flour, unsifted unbleached
2 cups sugar
½ teaspoon salt
½ teaspoon baking soda
1 teaspoon grated lemon peel
1 teaspoon vanilla
1 cup butter, softened
1 8-ounce cup yogurt, I recommend the stronger flavors
3 large eggs

Topping (or insert in middle): 1 cup chocolate chips, nuts or cinnamon–sugar mix. Consider adding on top of prepared batter, as a layer within batter or stirred into entire batter.

Lemon Glaze (optional)
1 cup powdered sugar
2 tablespoons lemon juice

DIRECTIONS
1. Preheat oven to 325° F. Grease and flour 10 inch Bundt or tube pan.
2. In a mixer, combine all ingredients. Blend at low speed until combined. Blend 3 minutes at medium speed. Pour into prepared pan. Consider toppings.
3. Bake for 60–70 minutes, until top springs back when lightly touched in center.
4. Cool cake upright in pan for 15 minutes. Remove from pan and cool completely.
5. In a small mixing bowl, combine powdered sugar and lemon juice to make a drizzle consistency. Place the glaze in a small plastic bag. Cut a very small corner of the bag and drizzle glaze on cooled cake. Ice cream on top is great.

Serves 10.

Chocolate Sauce

Kathy Alden

INGREDIENTS
¼ cup unsalted butter
2 ounces unsweetened chocolate
¾ cup sugar
2 tablespoons unsweetened cocoa powder
½ cup heavy cream
2 teaspoons vanilla extract

DIRECTIONS
1. Melt butter and chocolate together in a double boiler set over simmering water. In a separate bowl, combine sugar and cocoa. Stir the heavy cream into the sugar and cocoa and mix until a thick paste forms.
2. Stir the chocolate paste into the melted chocolate and butter. Cook mixture over simmering water for 5 minutes, stirring constantly. Remove from heat. Whisk in the vanilla and serve warm or at room temperature. Makes 1½ cups of sauce.

Rich *(but not too sweet)* Chocolate Cake *or Cupcakes*

Doug Kidder
Amherst College | Berkeley Paddling and Rowing Club

INGREDIENTS
½ cup hot water
5 ounces baking chocolate
1 cup butter, softened
2 cups sugar
4 eggs, separated
1 teaspoon vanilla
2½ cups cake flour
1 teaspoon baking soda
¼ teaspoon salt
⅔ cup yogurt
½ cup water
1 9 to 12-ounce package chocolate chips for cupcakes,
Frosting:
5 tablespoons butter, softened
1½ teaspoons vanilla
⅛ teaspoon salt
2–4 cups confectioners' sugar
Water

DIRECTIONS – Cake

1. Preheat oven to 350° F. Grease and flour either two 9 inch rounds or one 9 × 13 inch cake pan.
2. Put the chocolate in a microwave-safe bowl with the hot water. Heat in the microwave for a minute on high. Remove from oven and stir. Repeat heating and stirring until the chocolate is just melted and the whole bowl is a sort of a chocolate soup.
3. In a mixer, blend butter, sugar, egg yolks, chocolate soup and vanilla on medium speed until smooth.
4. In another bowl, sift the dry ingredients together.
5. In a third bowl, mix in yogurt and water.
6. Add the dry ingredients into the mixer along with the yogurt mix. Stir and mix until smooth without over mixing.

7. Whip egg whites until stiff. Fold the egg whites into the batter until egg whites are evenly spread throughout the batter. If adding chocolate chips, put them in the batter now.
8. Bake in prepared pan for 50 minutes or so. Cake is done when cake no longer leaves a dent when pressed down. Cake is done when springs back when touched.

Optional: Cook 24 cupcakes for 15 minutes. Mix chocolate chips into batter before pouring into cupcake tins.

DIRECTIONS – Frosting
In an electric mixing bowl, beat together the butter, vanilla salt and about ¼ cup of the confectioners sugar until smooth. Add approximately a cup of confectioners sugar and perhaps a tablespoon of water. Mix again until it is smooth. Keep adding confectioners sugar and water until enough frosting has been made. Add salt and vanilla to taste. Remember — it is better to have too much frosting than to have that awkward corner that didn't get any.

Serves 15.

Rustic Apple Tatin

Brenda Kieffer
Fairmont Rowing Association

INGREDIENTS

1 sweet piecrust or one packaged pie dough
½ cup marzipan
4 cups Granny Smith apples, sliced, peeled
¼ cup raisins or currants, rehydrated in some boiling water, drained and patted dry
½ cup granulated sugar
1 teaspoon all purpose flour
1 teaspoon almond extract, divided
2 teaspoons lemon juice
Zest from ½ lemon
Dash of salt
Syrup:
¼ cup granulated sugar
¼ cup water

DIRECTIONS

1. Preheat oven to 425° F. Line jellyroll pan *(baking sheet with sides)* with parchment.
2. Roll piecrust dough into a 14 inch circle *(don't worry if it is not a perfect circle, this is supposed to look rustic)*. Place dough on the parchment. Roll out marzipan into a smaller circle that leaves a 2–3 inch border of crust and place it on top of the dough.
3. In a bowl, combine apples, raisins, sugar, flour, ½ of the almond extract, lemon juice and zest. Toss until apples are well coated. Spoon apple mixture over dough and press up edges over the apples, so about a 2 inch border is formed. The finished product should look like a tire of filled dough with a circle of apples showing in the middle.
4. Bake for about 30 minutes until nicely browned.
5. When the apples are nearly done baking, make the syrup. In a heavy saucepan, heat sugar and water over med–high heat until the liquid begins to turn amber, stirring occasionally by watching carefully. Remove from the heat and add remaining almond extract. Immediately drizzle the syrup slowly over the tart.

Serves 10.

This tart is best made the day it is to be eaten, but will sit well for a few hours.

Coconut Pound Cake

Onie Rollins
Wilmington Rowing Center

INGREDIENTS

½ pound (2 sticks) butter
2¼ cups sugar
6 eggs
3 cups all-purpose flour
3½ cups shredded coconut

DIRECTIONS

1. Preheat oven to 325° F. Grease and flour tube pan.
2. In a mixer, cream butter & add sugar gradually. Incorporate eggs, then flour, add coconut and blend well.
3. Pour batter into prepared pan and bake for about 1½ to 2 hours. Set on rack to cool.

Serves 8–12.

Thrombosis Brownies

Bachelors Barge Club

INGREDIENTS

¾ cup butter
3 ounces unsweetened chocolate
3 ounces semi-sweet chocolate
3 eggs
1½ cups sugar
¾ cup flour
1½ cups miniature marshmallows

DIRECTIONS

1. Preheat oven to 350° F. Prepare pan: butter and line with wax paper a 9 × 13 inch pan.
2. Melt butter and both chocolates in a double boiler. Let cool slightly.
3. In a mixer, beat eggs until thick. Add sugar slowly while continuing to beat. Fold in flour and marshmallows. Add the melted chocolate mixture and fold in. Be gentle.
4. Pour the batter into prepared pan. Bake for 15 minutes, rotate pan and continue baking for 20 more minutes.

Makes 2 dozen brownies.

Chocolate Trifle

Izzie Brown *was a 2-time national team member and former assistant coach of Temple University's Women's Rowing Team*
Bachelors Barge Club | Berkeley Paddling and Rowing Club

INGREDIENTS
1 box deep chocolate cake mix (all ingredients as needed to make the cake)
½ cup Kahlúa
2 packages instant chocolate pudding
Milk as needed for pudding
1 large container frozen whipped topping
3 Skors or Heath candy bars, frozen, crushed into crumbs with rolling pin.

DIRECTIONS
1. Two days ahead, make cake as directed in 9 × 13 inch pan. Cool, leave in pan, cut into one inch squares.
2. Pour Kahlúa over cake, cover, refrigerate for two days. At this time, thaw frozen whipped topping in refrigerator.
3. On day of event, make pudding according to package.
4. In a trifle or tall clear glass bowl, layer half of chocolate cake squares in bowl. On cake layer ½ of chocolate pudding, ½ of whipped topping and ½ of crushed candy bars. Repeat all layers starting with cake.

Serves 16 chocolate lovers.

Belle's Best Oatmeal Chocolate Chip Cookies

Andrea Greeley – *Belle is a very sweet woman who worked at Sweenor's Chocolates during the daytime, when we University of Rhode Island rowers worked there in the evenings.*
Bachelors Barge Club

INGREDIENTS

1 cup butter
¾ cup brown sugar
¼ cup sugar
1 package instant vanilla pudding mix
2 eggs
1 teaspoon vanilla
1⅓ cup flour
1 teaspoon baking soda
3 cups 1-minute oats
1 12-ounce package chocolate chips

DIRECTIONS

1. Preheat oven to 350° F.
2. In a mixer, cream butter with both sugars and pudding mix. Add eggs and vanilla until combined. Add flour and baking soda until combined. Remove from mixer; add oats and chocolate chips, stirring with a big metal spoon (this is very thick — don't use a wooden or plastic spoon, I have broken many!)
3. Drop 1 tablespoon batter onto ungreased cookie sheet about 3 inches apart. Bake for about 10 minutes.

Makes 4–5 dozen cookies.

Apple Crisp

Mitz Carr
Crescent Boat Club | New Haven Rowing Club

INGREDIENTS
½ cup oatmeal
½ cup cranberries
½ cup pecans or walnuts, chopped and toasted
½ cup brown sugar
Zest of 1 lemon
1 teaspoon cinnamon
5 tablespoons butter, melted
4 large, OR 5 medium cooking apples: Pippin, McIntosh, or Granny Smith

DIRECTIONS
1. Preheat oven to 375° F. Butter a 9 × 9 inch baking dish.
2. In a large bowl, combine oatmeal, cranberries, nuts, brown sugar, lemon zest, cinnamon and butter.
3. Wash and core apples, leaving skin on, quarter, then slice the quarters so that ⅓ of slices can be arranged in two layers at bottom of baking dish. Sprinkle ⅓ of the oatmeal mixture over layer. Alternate apple and oatmeal mixture for another 2 layers ending with oatmeal mixture on top.
4. Place in oven for 25 minutes or until bubbling. Wait 15 minutes to serve.

Serves 4–5.

Pumpkin Soufflé

Ellen Braithwaite *who learned to row in Vermont where the water is flat, and the season short. Now she rows on the San Francisco Bay where the water is usually a little chaotic but the season is long. She loves it all, and the rowing world is a wonderful community to be a part of.*
Berkeley Paddling and Rowing Club | Open Water Rowing Center

INGREDIENTS

1 envelope gelatin
¼ cup rum
4 eggs
⅔ cup sugar
1 cup pumpkin
½ teaspoon cinnamon
½ teaspoon ginger
¼ teaspoon mace
¼ teaspoon cloves
1 cup heavy cream

DIRECTIONS

1. Dissolve the gelatin in the rum in the top of a double boiler (or in a small cup over hot water). Stir while it dissolves, and then let it sit while you do the next steps.
2. In a mixer, beat the eggs until frothy.
3. In a medium mixing bowl, mix the spices with the sugar and beat into the eggs. Add the pumpkin and the rum/gelatin mixture and mix well.
4. With an electric mixer, whip the cream until it's thick and fold it into the rest of the mixture.
5. Chill for about four hours.

Serves 6–8.

This is one of those family Thanksgiving recipes that exists on little scraps of paper, usually illegible, and so cousins and siblings tend to call each other up in a panic before the holiday. You can vary the spices, use maple syrup instead of sugar or use a substitute for the cream if you must. However you do it, it's a nice addition to the usual collection of Thanksgiving pies.

Peppermint Bark

Margaret Tobin – *Vesper Boat Club Gardener*

INGREDIENTS
2 cups chocolate chips
1½ cups white chocolate chips
1 cup leftover candy canes, smashed

DIRECTIONS
1. Preheat oven to 200° F. Using a baking pan with sides, line pan with aluminum foil.
2. Pour chocolate chips into prepared pan. Chips should cover entire pan one layer thick. Turn heat in oven off and place pan in hot oven for about 1 minute or until chips are melted.
3. Remove from oven and with a knife, spread into a thin layer. Cover chocolate layer with white chocolate chips. Return to hot oven until melted, about 1 minute. Spread into a second layer with knife.
4. Sprinkle with crushed candy canes.
5. Refrigerate until chocolate is no longer shiny, only a few minutes. Remove from refrigerator and break into large chunks. Enjoy. Great as gifts.

Makes 1 pan.

Bittersweet Chocolate Soufflés

Gabby Griffin
Bachelors Barge Club

INGREDIENTS

2 tablespoons granulated sugar to coat 8 4–5 ounce ramekin soufflé cups (optional)
¾ cup sugar, divided into ½ & ¼ cups
½ cup unsweetened cocoa, natural or Dutch processed
2 tablespoons flour
½ cup 1% milk
2 egg yolks
1 teaspoon pure vanilla extract
Pinch of salt
4 egg whites
⅛ teaspoon cream of tarter
3 ounces bittersweet chocolate, preferably 70%, finely chopped
About 1 tablespoon powdered sugar

DIRECTIONS

1. Preheat oven to 350° F with rack in the lower third.
2. Lightly grease the sides and bottom of the ramekins. If you are sugaring the cups, pour the sugar into one cup. Holding the cup over a second cup to catch any spills, tilt and rotate the sugar-filled cup until the bottom and sides are coated. Tap excess sugar into the second cup. Repeat until all the cups are coated, adding more sugar if necessary.
3. In a small saucepan, combine the cocoa and flour with ½ cup of the sugar. Stir in enough of the milk for a smooth paste. Stir in the remaining milk. Heat slowly, stirring constantly until the mixture bubbles slightly around the edges of the pan. Continue to cook and stir until the mixture is slightly thickened, about 2 minutes, scraping the bottom and sides of the pan to avoid scorching.
4. Scrape the hot mixture into a large bowl. Whisk in egg yolks, vanilla and salt. Set aside.
5. In a separate, clean dry mixing bowl, beat 4 egg whites with the cream of tarter at medium speed until soft peaks form when the beater is lifted. Add the remaining ¼ cup of sugar gradually, continuing to beat at high speed until the egg whites are stiff but not dry.

6. Fold about ¼ of the egg whites into the chocolate mixture to lighten it. Scrape the remaining egg whites into the chocolate mixture and fold several strokes until the egg whites are partially blended. Sprinkle in the chopped chocolate and fold until the egg whites and chocolate are blended. Divide the mixture between the 8 cups filling them nearly full.
7. Either bake immediately or refrigerate in cups for up to a day. Cold soufflés will take up to a minute or two to bake. If baking immediately, place filled ramekins on a cookie sheet and bake for 15–16 minutes. Soufflés are done when they puff up above the rim of the cup, crack on top and a toothpick inserted in the center emerges with creamy thick batter still clinging to it. Do not over bake. Sieve powdered sugar over the tops and serve immediately.

Serves 8.

Carmel Choco-Squares

Bachelors Barge Club

INGREDIENTS

About 50 light caramels, 14-ounce package
⅔ cup evaporated milk, divided in half
1 box German chocolate cake mix
¾ cup butter, melted
1 cup chopped nuts (optional)
1 cup semi-sweet chocolate chips, 6-ounce package

DIRECTIONS

1. In the top of a double boiler, combine caramels and ⅓ cup evaporated milk. Cook over hot water, stirring constantly, until caramels melt. Set aside.
2. Preheat oven to 350° F. Generously grease and lightly flour a 13 × 9 inch baking pan.
3. In a large bowl, combine dry cake mix, butter, ⅓ cup evaporated milk and nuts. Stir by hand until dough holds together.
4. Press ½ of dough into prepared pan. Bake for 6 minutes.
5. Sprinkle chocolate pieces over baked crust. Spread caramel mixture over chocolate pieces. Crumble remaining dough over caramel mixture.
6. Return to oven and bake for 18–22 minutes. Cool slightly, refrigerate for about 30 minutes to set caramel layer. Cut into bars.

Makes 36 bars.

Gingerbread Cider Cake

Malta Boat Club

INGREDIENTS
2 cups all purpose flour
1½ teaspoons baking soda
1¼ teaspoons ground ginger or 1 tablespoon fresh chopped ginger
1 teaspoon cinnamon
½ teaspoon salt
¼ teaspoon cloves, ground
¼ teaspoon nutmeg
1 stick butter
½ cup sugar
1 large egg
1 cup molasses
1 cup water
Topping:
¾ cup brown sugar
1½ cups apple cider or juice
2 tablespoon butter, melted

DIRECTIONS
1. Preheat oven to 350° F. Use ungreased 9 × 13 inch pan.
2. In a medium mixing bowl, combine flour, baking soda, ginger, cinnamon, salt, cloves and nutmeg.
3. In a small bowl, combine molasses and water.
4. In a large mixing bowl, cream butter and white sugar with hand held mixer, about 1 to 2 minutes. Add egg and mix well. Add flour mixture in 3 additions, alternating with molasses mixture. Mix until just blended.
5. Pour batter into ungreased pan. Sprinkle batter with the brown sugar.
6. Heat the cider and melted butter. Pour over top of batter.
7. Bake until cracked on top and toothpick comes out clean, about 40–45 minutes.

Serves 24.

Spanish Bread Pudding

Maria Dreher
Malta Boat Club

INGREDIENTS
1 king-size loaf of bread, 22oz
3 eggs
1 ¼ cups of sugar
2 tsp. vanilla
2 teaspoons cinnamon
1 can of evaporated milk
1 can of water, refill evaporated milk can with the water
1 cup raisins
1 stick butter, melted, divided ¾ and ¼

DIRECTIONS
1. Preheat oven at 325° F. Pour ¼ of butter into 9 × 13 inch pan and coat.
2. In a medium bowl, mix eggs, sugar, vanilla, cinnamon, milk, and water together. Add raisins and stir. Mix in ¾ of the butter after it has cooled.
3. In a large mixing bowl, break up the bread into 1 inch chunks. Pour the wet mixture over the bread. Break down mixture with hands into a pudding consistency.
4. Pour mixture into prepared pan and bake for 1 hour. Cool and enjoy!

Serves 20.

The pudding is great with a dollop of whipped cream and caramel drizzle.

Opa Koerner's Dutch Plum Cake

Opa Koerner

INGREDIENTS

1 cup all purpose flour, sifted
1½ teaspoons baking powder
½ teaspoon salt
1 tablespoon granulated sugar
¼ cup butter
1 egg
¼ cup milk
16 small plums, pitted and cut in half
Topping:
½ teaspoon cinnamon
¼ teaspoon nutmeg
2 tablespoon granulated sugar
2 tablespoon butter, melted
½ cup currant jelly or apricot jam

DIRECTIONS

1. Preheat oven to 400° F. Grease 8 × 12 inch baking dish.
2. In a large bowl, sift together 1 cup flour, baking powder, salt and sugar. Cut in butter using 2 knives or pastry blender, until texture of course corn meal.
3. In a separate bowl, combine egg and milk. Stir into dry ingredients with fork. Spread in prepared baking dish. Arrange plums, skin side up, slightly overlapping in parallel rows on top with fruit pushed halfway into dough.
4. Make topping in a small bowl by combining cinnamon, nutmeg and 2 tablespoons sugar. Sprinkle over fruit. Top with melted butter.
5. Bake for 40–45 minutes, until plums are tender. Remove from oven. Beat jelly with fork and spread on top.

Makes 8 × 12 inch pan.

Cheese Cake

Malta Boat Club

INGREDIENTS

3 packages cream cheese
3 eggs
Juice of ½ lemon
1 teaspoon vanilla
1 teaspoon baking powder
1¼ cup sugar
2 Graham Cracker pie crusts
⅓ cup cherry pie filling (optional)

DIRECTIONS

1. Preheat oven to 325° F.
2. In a mixer, combine cream cheese, eggs, lemon juice, vanilla, baking powder, and sugar until smooth.
3. Pour ½ mixture into each graham cracker pie shell. If desired, swirl half of cherry pie filling in each pie.
4. Bake for 1 hour.

Makes 2 pies.

Orange Dream Fruit Salad

From www.recipe.com

Renee Sutton
Wilmington Rowing Center

INGREDIENTS

3 cups seeded, peeled, and chopped mangoes or papayas
4 11-ounce cans mandarin orange sections, drained
3 cups seedless red and/or green grapes, halved
2 8-ounce containers orange-flavored yogurt, low fat, if desired
1 teaspoon poppy seeds
2 cups fresh blueberries

DIRECTIONS

1. In a very large bowl, combine the mangoes or papayas, drained oranges, and grapes.
2. In a medium bowl, stir together the yogurt and poppy seeds.
3. Gently stir yogurt mixture into the fruit mixture until combined.
4. Cover and chill up to 6 hours.
5. Stir in blueberries just before serving.

Serves 25.

Annamarie's Jewish Apple Cake

Malta Boat Club

INGREDIENTS

5 or 6 apples, peeled, cut in chunks
2 teaspoons cinnamon
5 tablespoons sugar
Batter:
3 cups flour
2 cups sugar
1 cup canola oil
4 eggs
¼ cup orange juice
3 teaspoons baking powder
2½ teaspoons vanilla
1 teaspoons salt

DIRECTIONS

1. Preheat oven to 350° F. Grease and flour Bundt or tube pan.
2. In a medium mixing bowl, combine peeled and chunked apples, cinnamon and 5 tablespoons sugar. Set aside.
3. In a large mixing bowl make batter by combining flour, 2 cups sugar, oil, eggs, orange juice, baking powder, vanilla and salt.
4. Pour ½ of batter into prepared pan. Spread half the apple mixture on top of batter, cover with remaining batter, and top with remaining of apples.
5. Bake for 1½ hours. Remove from pan and cool on rack.

Makes 1 Bundt cake.

Crumb Cake

Doug Kidder
Berkeley Paddling and Rowing Club

INGREDIENTS
2 cups flour
¾ cup sugar
1 teaspoon baking powder
½ teaspoon baking soda
Pinch of salt
⅓ cup butter
1 egg
¾ cup water
1 teaspoon vanilla
Topping:
½ teaspoon cinnamon
¼ teaspoon cloves, ground
⅓ cup brown sugar
2 teaspoons butter

DIRECTIONS
1. Preheat the oven to 350° F. Butter 9 inch round cake pan.
2. In a big bowl, sift together flour, sugar, baking powder, baking soda and salt. Chop the butter in with a pastry blender until the bits of dough are the size of peas. Reserve ¼ cup mixture for topping.
3. Add the egg, water and vanilla to the flour and butter mixture. Mix just until blended. Pour into prepared pan.
4. In a small bowl, combine cinnamon, cloves, sugar, butter and flour mixture reserved earlier. Chop and mix until the bits of butter are the size of peas or smaller.
5. Spread the topping over the top of the batter. Bake for 25 minutes.

Serves 6.

This is a long time favorite recipe. We eat it for breakfast, brunch and as dessert. It is quick and easy to make and can be made with only a bowl, a dull knife and a spoon so I've made it everywhere from apartments in Hong Kong to camps in Maine.

Best Chocolate Chip Cookies Ever

Sheri Sullivan & Susan May
Bachelors Barge Club

INGREDIENTS
2 sticks of butter
½ cup granulated sugar
½ cup brown sugar
2 teaspoons vanilla extract
2 eggs
1 cup Old Fashioned Quaker Oats, ground
1⅛ to 1¼ cup regular flour
⅛ teaspoon salt, or a little less
1 teaspoon baking soda
1½ cup chocolate chips

DIRECTIONS
1. In a mixer, cream butter. Mix both sugars until smooth and creamy. Add vanilla extract and mix. Add eggs and mix. Set aside.
2. Grind enough Old Fashioned Quaker Oats with a coffee grinder or other kitchen device to make 1 cup of flour. Lightly tamp down flour into measuring cup as the grinder fluffs up the flour a lot. In a smaller bowl, combine ground oats, flour, salt and baking soda. Mix ingredients well.
3. Add flour mixture to egg mixture slowly and mix. Turn off mixer as soon as 95% of the flour mixture has been incorporated. Remove from mixer and stir in chocolate chips by hand, stirring as little as possible.
4. Using an ice cream scooper (the kind with a trigger release), place scoops of batter tightly together on a baking sheet to freeze. Flatten them slightly with the back of the spoon. When frozen, place in a Ziploc bag. Freezing or refrigerating the cookies before baking improves the texture and look of the cookies. Do not thaw before baking. Cookies can be baked without freezing. In that case, do not flatten batter.
5. Bake at 375° F for 9–11 minutes, depending on your oven.

Makes about 5 dozen cookies.

Ginger Cookies

Murray Callahan Blackwall
University Barge Club

INGREDIENTS
1 cup dark brown sugar
1 cup granulated sugar
1 cup molasses, blackstrap preferred
1 cup butter, melted for chewier cookies
2 eggs
3 cups flour
½ teaspoon salt
3 level teaspoons baking powder
1½ teaspoons clove, ground
1½ teaspoons ginger, ground
2 teaspoons cinnamon, ground
10x sugar, replenish as needed

DIRECTIONS
1. Preheat oven to 375° F.
2. In a mixer, blend brown and granulated sugars, molasses, butter and eggs.
3. In a small bowl, sift together flour, salt, baking powder, clove, ginger and cinnamon. Gradually add the dry ingredients to the wet — dough will be sticky. Roll dough into a cylinder in plastic wrap and refrigerate for at least 1 hour — or freeze indefinitely.
4. Cut and roll dough into walnut sized balls and bake on a greased cookie sheet (or parchment paper on a cookie sheet) for 8 to 10 minutes, turning pan at 8 minutes.
5. Remove oven and let cool until they can be lifted from pan easily. Place on a cooling rack or other sheet, cool for a few minutes, then drop a few baked cookies into a bag of 10x sugar to coat. Repeat with remaining cookies. Cool the cookie sheets between batches or the cookies will run.

Makes 4–5 dozen cookies.

Blueberry Clafoutis

Margaret Meigs
University Barge Club

INGREDIENTS

1¼ cup flour
¾ cup sugar
1 stick butter
½ teaspoon cinnamon
½ teaspoon salt
¼ teaspoon baking powder
1½ pints blueberries or raspberries
¾ cup cream or half and half
½ teaspoon vanilla
1 egg

DIRECTIONS

1. Preheat oven to 375° F. Butter a tart pan.In a food processor, combine flour, sugar, butter, cinnamon, salt and baking powder. Pulse until the consistency of coarse crumbs. Reserving ⅓ cup for later.
2. Press dough into prepared pan.
3. In a bowl, gently mix the berries with the reserved dough and place the mixture onto crust.
4. Bake for 15 minutes. While baking, beat together the cream, vanilla and egg. Remove tart from heat, pour cream mixture over berries and return to oven for an additional 20–25 minutes. Remove from oven and let cool.

Serves 6–8.

Nice when served with a dollop of vanilla ice cream.

John Paynich's Gluten-Free Easy Peanut Butter Cookies

Margaret Tobin – *Vesper Boat Club Gardener*

INGREDIENTS
1 cup peanut butter
1 cup sugar, extra for crispy cookie tops
1 egg
Crunchy peanut butter, chocolate chips, raisins, dried fruit, granola (optional)

DIRECTIONS
1. Preheat oven to 350° F.
2. In a mixing bowl, combine peanut butter, sugar and egg. Beat until well combined and fluffy.
3. Drop dough by teaspoons on an ungreased cookie sheet. For crispy tops: dip fork tines in sugar and make a fork tine imprint by pressing fork down into dough. Repeat sugar and pressing with tines of the fork in the opposite direction.
4. Bake for 10 minutes. Eat. Enjoy!

Makes 2 dozen cookies.

Stocks, Sauces & Dressings

Bouquet Garni

A bundle of herbs tied together with a string. Herbs vary depending on the recipe.

INGREDIENTS
1 bay leaf
3 sprigs thyme
4 large sprigs parsley (including stalks)
4 inch piece celery stalked with leaves
2 4 inch pieces leek, use green part

DIRECTIONS
Place the bay leaf, thyme, parsley and celery on one piece of green leek. Cover with the remaining piece of green leek. Tie securely with fine string, leaving a length of string attached so that the bouquet garni can be easily retrieved.

Chicken Stock

INGREDIENTS
1 carcass from whole turkey or chicken
1 tablespoon vegetable oil
1 large onion, quartered with skin on
2 large celery stalks, with leaves, cut into 1 inch pieces
2 large carrots, cut into 1 inch pieces
1 bouquet garni
3 quarts water

DIRECTIONS
In large stockpot over medium heat, add oil and sauté onions, celery and carrots for about five minutes or until just beginning to brown. Add chicken, bouquet garni and water; bring to a boil. Skim off any foam that rises. Reduce heat and simmer gently, uncovered, for two to three hours. Strain out solids through cheesecloth in a colander and return to smaller pot. Place in refrigerator over night and remove gelled fat. Return to heat and simmer another hour or so until reduced by half. Salt to taste.

Beef Stock

INGREDIENTS
2 pounds beef bones or beef trimmings
1 small can tomato paste
1 tablespoon canola oil
1 large onion, skin on, quartered
2 large stalks celery, cut into 1 inch pieces
2 large carrots, cut into 1 inch pieces
1 bouquet garni
3 quarts water

DIRECTIONS
Preheat oven to 375° F. Rub tomato paste generously over bones. Roast bones in roasting pan for about 30 minutes until browned. In large stockpot over medium heat, add oil and sauté onions, celery and carrots for about 5 minutes. Add bones and bouquet garni and bring to a boil. Skim off any foam. Reduce heat and simmer uncovered for 2–3 hours. Strain through fine strainer and return to a smaller pot. Skim fat. Return to medium heat and simmer another hour or so until reduced by half. Salt to taste.

Vegetable Stock

INGREDIENTS
2 teaspoons olive oil
3 cups each:
  onion, garlic, celery, carrot, tomato, mushroom, chopped into 1 inch pieces
1 bouquet garni
1 quart water

DIRECTIONS
Heat oil in 2-quart saucepan. Add onion, garlic, celery and carrots. Sauté until onions are translucent but not browned. Add remaining vegetables, bouquet garni and water. Bring to a boil, the reduce heat and gently simmer uncovered for 45 to 60 minutes. Salt to taste. Strain liquid through a colander. Return to heat and reduce liquid by about half or to taste. Should yield about 1 pint stock.

White Sauce

INGREDIENTS
2 tablespoons butter
2 tablespoons flour
1 cup milk

DIRECTIONS
Melt butter over medium low heat. Stir in flour and heat for 1 minute to form a roux. Remove from heat and whisk in ¼ cup milk. Return to heat and stir until mixture thickens. Gradually add remainder of milk while stirring gently. Increase heat slowly until mixture boils. Reduce heat and simmer gently for about five minutes, whisking occasionally, to cook flour.

Brown Sauce

INGREDIENTS
2 tablespoons butter OR pan drippings
1 small carrot, diced
1 small onion, diced
¼ cup flour
2½ cups beef stock
Salt and pepper

DIRECTIONS
Melt butter or pan drippings over medium heat in saucepan. Add vegetables and sauté until lightly browned. Add flour to make a roux, lower heat and cook roux mixture until it turns light brown. Add the stock and bring to a boil, stirring constantly until sauce thickens. Strain to remove vegetables and any lumps. Salt and pepper to taste.

Gravy

INGREDIENTS

Pan drippings
2 tablespoons flour
2–4 tablespoons wine, broth OR stock

DIRECTIONS

Pour all cooking pan juices into a fat separator to remove excess fat. Return juices to pan over medium heat, add a few tablespoons of stock or wine and scrape up any browned bits. Add enough liquid to make appropriate number of servings and bring to a simmer. In a covered container, combine flour and 2 tablespoons water. Shake together until creamy. Slowly add flour mixture to simmering liquid, stirring continuously, until desired thickness is achieved. Simmer slowly for 5 minutes to cook flour.

Pan Sauce *or Deglazing Sauce*

INGREDIENTS

Pan drippings
2–4 tablespoons wine, broth OR stock

DIRECTIONS

Remove fat from warm pan drippings using a fat separator or baster and return liquid to the pan. Add a few tablespoons of wine, broth, stock or water. Scrape the pan to loosen browned bits. The resulting liquid becomes an instant sauce.

Marinara Sauce

INGREDIENTS
2 tablespoons olive oil
1 clove garlic
1 28-ounce can crushed tomatoes
2 tablespoons tomato paste
1 teaspoon parsley, minced
1 tablespoon fresh oregano
1 tablespoon fresh basil
1 teaspoon sugar
Salt and pepper

DIRECTIONS
Heat oil in saucepan over medium heat until hot. Add garlic and stir to coat, about 30 seconds. Do not let garlic brown. Add tomatoes, tomato paste, parsley, oregano, basil and sugar. Return to a simmer and cook for about 30 minutes. Salt and pepper to taste.

Pesto Sauce

INGREDIENTS
½ cup olive oil
1½ cups basil, fresh
2 cloves garlic, crushed and chopped
2 tablespoons pine nuts
½ cup Parmesan cheese, grated
2 tablespoons cream, heavy or half and half

DIRECTIONS
Place all ingredients except cream, in a food processor and process until creamy. For a more opaque and tastier pesto, add cream and process 10 seconds more. Serve over pasta.

Alfredo Sauce

INGREDIENTS

2 tablespoons butter
1 tablespoon flour
1½ cups cream, heavy or half and half
3 tablespoons Parmesan cheese, grated
Salt and pepper

DIRECTIONS

Heat butter in a saucepan. Combine flour to form a roux. Add cream and stir until in begins to thicken. Add cheese and nutmeg and continue to stir until desired consistency is achieved. Salt and pepper to taste. Variations: use Cheddar cheese to make a rich macaroni and cheese sauce.

Salsa

INGREDIENTS

1 quart water
1 tablespoon salt
3 tomatoes, finely chopped
5 peppers, seeded and finely chopper (Serrano, Jalapeño, chili — red or green)
2 cloves garlic, chopped
½ cup onion, chopped
½ cup cilantro or parsley
3 tablespoons olive oil
Salt and pepper

DIRECTIONS

In a saucepan over high heat, add water and salt and bring to a boil. Add chopped tomatoes and peppers. Cook uncovered until soft, about 10 minutes. Discard water. Place softened vegetables along with garlic, onion, herbs and oil in a food processor or blender and pulse until roughly chopped. Adjust salt and pepper to taste. Let cool and serve.

Cole Slaw Dressing

INGREDIENTS
½ cup mayonnaise
¼ cup sour cream
3 teaspoons vinegar or lemon juice
1 tablespoon prepared mustard
1 tablespoon sugar
½ teaspoon celery seed
Salt and pepper

DIRECTIONS
Combine all in a bowl and season to taste. Add shredded cabbage and mix.

Italian Dressing

INGREDIENTS
1 cup olive oil
¼ cup vinegar
1 clove garlic, minced
Dash each salt, pepper and mustard
2 tablespoons onion, minced
1 teaspoon basil, dried
½ teaspoon oregano, dried
¼ teaspoon peppercorns, cracked
2 cloves garlic, finely minced
1 teaspoon sugar

DIRECTIONS
Shake all ingredients in tightly covered container. For creamy Italian dressing add ½ cup mayonnaise.

Herb Dressing

INGREDIENTS
1 cup olive oil
¼ cup vinegar
1 clove garlic, minced
Dash salt
Dash pepper
Dash mustard
2 tablespoons green onion, finely minced
½ teaspoon parsley, fresh, minced
¼ teaspoon each tarragon, rosemary, basil, oregano and thyme
¼ teaspoons pepper corns, cracked
2 cloves garlic, finely minced
1 teaspoon sugar

DIRECTIONS
Shake all ingredients in tightly covered container.

Kitchen Helper

Equivalents

INGREDIENT	QUANTITY	YIELD
Almonds	1 pound with shells	1 cup shelled
Beans	1 cup dry	2½–3 cups cooked
Bread	2 slices	1 cup soft crumbs
Butter	2 tablespoons	1 ounce
Butter	1 stick	½ cup (8 tablespoons)
Carrots	1 pound fresh	3 cups diced
Celery	1 pound fresh	4 cups diced
Chocolate Chips	6 ounces	1 cup
Corn	3 ears	1 cup kernels
Flour	1 pound	4 cups
Garlic	1 clove	½ teaspoon minced
Lemon	1 medium	3–4 teaspoon juice OR 1 teaspoon zest
Onion	1 medium	½ cup minced
Peas, *in pod*	1 pound	1 cup cooked
Potatoes	1 pound (3 medium)	2½ cups diced
Rice	1 cup dry	4 cups cooked
Strawberries	1 pint	2 cups sliced
Sugar, *powdered*	1 pound	4 cups
Sugar, *granulated*	1 pound	2 cups
Tomatoes	1 medium	1 cup chopped
Walnuts	1 pound with shells	2 cups shelled
Zucchini	1 medium	2 cups sliced

Dry Measure Conversion

⅟48 CUP	⅟16 FL.OZ	⅓ TBSP	1 TSP	0.075 ML
⅟16 CUP	½ FL.OZ	1 TBSP	3 TSP	15 ML
⅛ CUP	1 FL.OZ	2 TBSP	6 TSP	30 ML
¼ CUP	2 FL.OZ	4 TBSP	12 TSP	59 ML
⅓ CUP	2⅔ FL.OZ	5⅓ TBSP	16 TSP	79 ML
½ CUP	4 FL.OZ	8 TBSP	24 TSP	118 ML
⅔ CUP	5⅓ FL.OZ	10⅔ TBSP	32 TSP	158 ML
¾ CUP	6 FL.OZ	12 TBSP	36 TSP	177 ML
1 CUP	8 FL.OZ	16 TBSP	48 TSP	237 ML

Substitutions

IF YOU DON'T HAVE ANY	TRY THIS
Bread crumbs, *1 cup*	¾ to 1 cup cracker crumbs
Buttermilk, *1 cup*	1 cup warm milk + 1 tablespoon vinegar or lemon juice.
Baking powder, *1 teaspoon*	¼ teaspoon baking soda + ½ teaspoon cream of tartar
Broth, *1 cup*	1 cup water + 1 bullion cube or 1 teaspoon granules
Chocolate, *unsweetened*	Baking cocoa + 1 tablespoon butter
Cornstarch, *1 teaspoon*	2 teaspoons flour
Corn syrup, *1 cup light*	1¼ cup granulated sugar + ¼ cup water
Half and half, *1 cup*	1½ tablespoons butter + enough whole milk to equal 1 cup
Sour cream, *1 cup*	1 cup yogurt or 1 tablespoon lemon juice + enough evaporated milk to make 1 cup
Lemon juice, *1 tablespoon*	½ tablespoon vinegar
Prepared mustard, *1 tablespoon*	1 teaspoon dry mustard
Pumpkin spice, *1 teaspoon*	½ teaspoon cinnamon, ¼ teaspoon ground ginger, and a pinch each of nutmeg and all spice
Dark brown sugar, *1 cup*	1 cup granulated sugar + 2 tablespoons molasses or dark corn syrup
Yogurt, *1 cup*	1 cup milk + 1 tablespoon lemon juice, let stand five minutes

Liquid Measure Conversion

				½ FL.OZ	0.015 L	1 TBSP	3 TSP
			⅛ CUP	1 FL.OZ	0.03 L	2 TBSP	6 TSP
			¼ CUP	2 FL.OZ	0.06 L	4 TBSP	12 TSP
			½ CUP	4 FL.OZ	0.12 L	8 TBSP	24 TSP
	¼ QT	½ PT	1 CUP	8 FL.OZ	0.24 L		
	½ QT	1 PT	2 CUPS	16 FL.OZ	0.47 L		
¼ GAL	1 QT	2 PT	4 CUPS	32 FL.OZ	0.95 L		
½ GAL	2 QT	4 PT	8 CUPS	64 FL.OZ	1.89 L		
1 GAL	4 QT	8 PT	16 CUPS	128 FL.OZ	3.79 L		

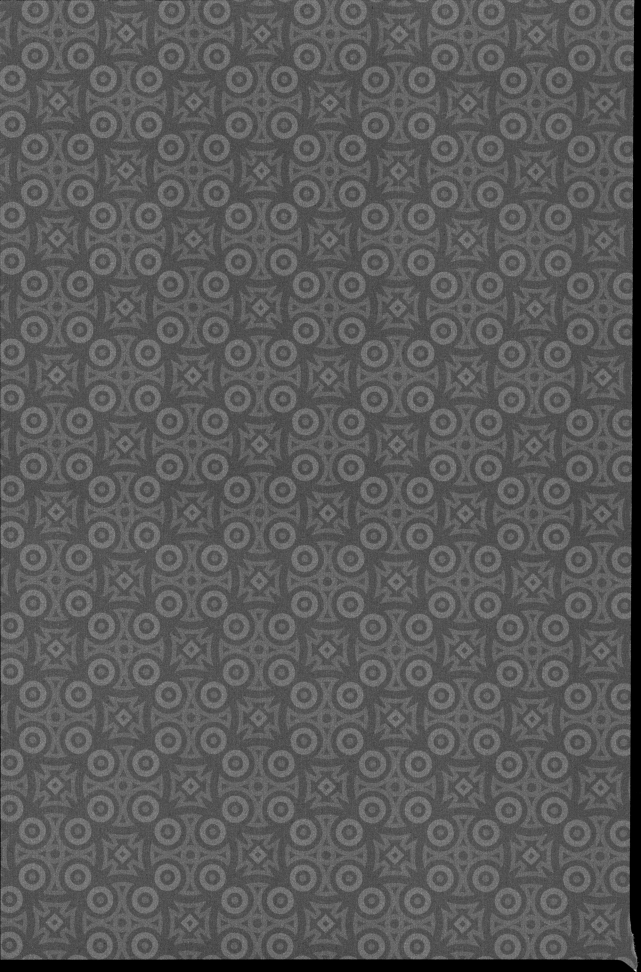

Izzie Brown is a professor of sports nutrition at San Jose State University. As a Registered Dietitian with a Master's Degree in Exercise Science, she has extensively studied the sport of rowing. A rower since 1981, Izzie rowed for six years along Boathouse Row as an elite athlete. She continues to row daily in Berkeley, CA in her single and in a double. She and her rowing partner are inspired by the thirty-year rowing partnership of Fred Duling and Rick Stehlik.

About Fred, Izzie says, "Fred has been like a second dad to me. During times when I was struggling, Fred was a friend who provided a safe place to belong. His warm and somewhat sarcastic sense of humor always added levity to the dreaded race weigh-ins."

Izzie's motivation in creating the Boathouse Row Cookbook was to raise money for Fred's health care expenses. She also hopes the proceeds will go toward making Fred's beloved Malta Boat Club and a launch wheelchair accessible so he can get back to coaching.

This book was designed and set into type by Ozan Berke at designerDad studios in Oakland.

The text face is Minion, designed by Robert Slimbach in 1990. The name comes from the traditional naming system for type sizes, in which minion is between nonpareil and brevier. It is inspired by late Renaissance-era type.

Made in the USA
Monee, IL
18 January 2021